PRAISE FOR
LAKE *of the* PRAIRIES

"Warren Cariou is humorous while always being thoughful, and his descriptive power is exceptional. He is one of the very best young writers of our time."
—Alistair MacLeod, author of *No Great Mischief*

"Cariou's writing achieves everything great art should aim to do. It finds something basic and universal in all of us, the beautiful and the profane, and gracefully delivers us to a more enlightened understanding of the relationships that bless and haunt us all."
—Dennis Bock, author of *The Ash Garden*

"*Lake of the Prairies* is a fine addition to our literature of exile and belonging. This book arrives as a welcome balm for the wounds we experience as a nation that continues to abandon its rural routes (and roots). Cariou's narrative, with its abundant humour, humanity and humility, quickens the old and poignant truths that have always attended our wanderings away from home and back again."
—Trevor Herriot, author of *River in a Dry Land*

"This memoir is beautifully crafted, artful in its construction, and, as with all good memoirs, is, in the end, truly penetrating in its analysis-by-hindsight. . . . His evocation of this historic area of forests, marshes, muskeg and lakes reveals a world we otherwise would not have been fortunate enough to know."
—Sharon Butala, author of *The Perfection of the Morning*

"A superb book, and an honest one too. It is also a gentle book, a humane work that is enlightened and powered by the kind of understanding which can benefit us all."
—*The Edmonton Journal*

"Meadow Lake is now officially on the Canadian literary map, and so is Warren Cariou."
—*The Globe and Mail*

LAKE *of the* PRAIRIES

LAKE

of the

PRAIRIES

A Story of Belonging

WARREN CARIOU

ANCHOR CANADA

Copyright © Warren Cariou 2002
Anchor Canada edition 2003

Anchor Canada and colophon are trademarks.

National Library of Canada Cataloguing in Publication

Cariou, Warren, 1966–
    Lake of the Prairies : a story of belonging / Warren Cariou. — Anchor Canada ed.

ISBN 0-385-25961-1

1. Cariou, Warren, 1966– —Childhood and youth. 2. Cariou, Warren, 1966– —Family. 3. Lake of the Prairies Region (Man. and Sask.)— Biography. 4. Meadow Lake (Sask.)--Biography. 5. Authors, Canadian (English)—20th century—Biography. I. Title.

PS8555.A736Z53 2003   C813'.54   C2002-904250-X
PR9199.3.C33Z467 2003

Cover images courtesy of the author
Cover design: CS Richardson
Map: Weldon Hiebert
Text design: Carla Kean
Printed and bound in Canada

Unless specified otherwise, all text photos are courtesy of the author.

Published in Canada by
Anchor Canada, a division of
Random House of Canada Limited

Visit Random House of Canada Limited's website: www.randomhouse.ca

TRANS 10 9 8 7 6 5 4 3 2 1

For all the relations

A place is a story told many times.
— KIM STAFFORD

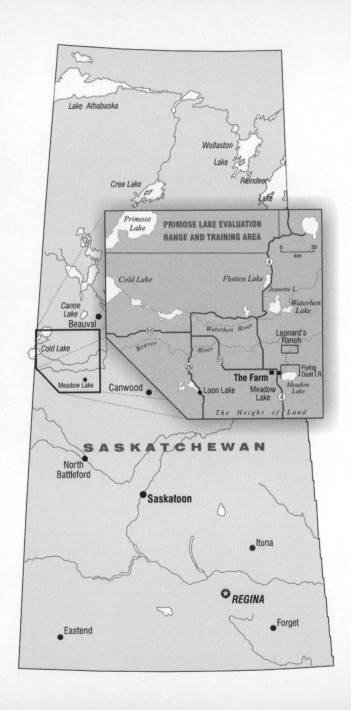

PRIMOSE LAKE EVALUATION
RANGE AND TRAINING AREA

Primose
Lake

0   20
km

4

Cold Lake

Flotten Lake

Jeanette L.

Waterhen
Lake

Waterhen River

Leonard's
Ranch

Beaver

River

55

26

55

The Farm

Flying
Dust I.R.

Loon Lake

Meadow
Lake

Meadow
Lake

4

The Height of Land

Lake Athabaska

Wollaston
Lake

Cree Lake

Reindeer

Lake

Canoe
Lake

Beauval

Cold Lake

Meadow Lake

Canwood

SASKATCHEWAN

North
Battleford

Saskatoon

Ituna

★ REGINA

Eastend

Forget

I

෨

The Story of You

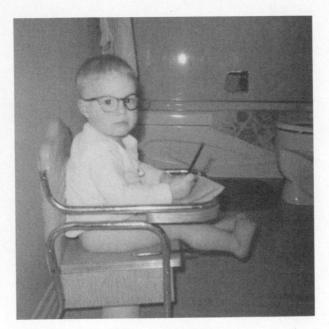

The writer at work.

ONCE UPON *a* TOWN

Where do I come from?

> *The potato patch.*
> *God in Heaven.*
> *A falling star.*
> *The stork.*
> *A moonlit night.*
> *A hole in the legs.*
> *You were named for the doctor who delivered you.*

Where, really?

> *From here. You're from right here. The town of*
> *Meadow Lake, the province of Saskatchewan, the*
> *country of Canada, the planet of Earth. Just down*
> *the street at the Meadow Lake Union Hospital you*
> *were born, and we lived in the Carter Apartments*
> *until you were one, and then we moved to the house,*
> *and you grew like quackgrass in the backyard.*
> *And that's the story of you.*

We always have to take someone's word for it, that mystery of origins. Maybe that's why I believed I was not so much from a place as from a story—or rather a collection of stories, mutually contradictory and continually evolving in the mouths of my many relatives. This was fine with me. I loved all stories. Dad told us new ones every night at bedtime, and sometimes during the day too, if we badgered him long enough. And even without such prompting, Uncle Hank and Uncle Vic and Uncle Leo told stories on each other, and then Dad would step in to contradict them all and we wouldn't know who to believe. Mom would stretch Dad's name out to two syllables—"Ra-ay!"—whenever she thought the shenanigans had gone too far, and Dad would say "Hmp. What! It's true!" in a tone that suggested the opposite. Dad and his brothers told their stories the way they played cards: as if there was a nickel at stake—and *that mattered*—and as if the others might very well be cheating. And the point, it seemed to me, was not to get at the truth but to trump their opponents with the most outrageous lie at the most opportune moment.

The household could break into these word-wars at the slightest provocation. One brother might say, "Does it seem cool in here to you?" and another would respond, "Naahhh. Not like those times at the farm when the water froze in the wash basin."

And the battle was on.

"Not like when *I* had to tunnel through eight-foot snowdrifts to get from the house to the chicken coop."

"Bullshit! It wasn't cold then. Snow's an insulator."

"Damn near smothered us though, right along with the chickens. I remember they were all keeled over when I got the door open, and the first thing I thought was, that damn weasel's back!"

"Weasel, indeed."

"*You* never did that tunnelling anyway. Uncle Corentin did—I remember him coming in with the shovel frozen to his mitts."

"I froze my ears in bed once, on the farm. Forgot to wear my tuque."

"Remember when the chickadees froze solid on the bob-wire fence?"

"That was your noggin that froze solid."

"They did. A dozen chickadees and a pigeon."

"And a great big clump of bull shit!"

"They did! I plucked them off like apples and Mom baked them in a pie."

"Ra-ay!"

We never knew how these jousts would end—with shouted accusations of bullshit, or laughter, or simmering silences that might well evolve into feuds. As a spectator sport, it was better than *Stampede Wrestling*, more suspense-ful than *The Edge of Night*.

When it was just the five of us, the immediate family, the stories were not so much a competition as a reward for good behaviour, or at least a diversion from bad.

"Tell us a story, Dad," we pleaded, several times a day.

"We'll see," he said. This was what he always said when we asked for anything. Once I asked if we could have an elephant to play with in our backyard sandbox and he said, "We'll see." Most of the time we didn't believe he was listening at all. But still we asked our questions, made our requests. It was part of the game, that we would try to coax him away from his newspaper or his book or his chesterfield snoozes. Usually when we had all but given up, he would turn to Glenn or me and say—as if the idea had just occurred to him—"Ready for a story, Buzz?"

He called both of us Buzz, short for Buzzard. Also Little Man. When Michelle was old enough to be something other than The Baby, she became Missy or Miss. And Glenn was Glenn D., and I was Warren G., which became Warren Jeremiah, even though my middle name was Gerald. Sometimes I wondered where these names had come from, but I didn't ask. It seemed appropriate that, just as there were multiple versions of my uncles' stories, there were multiple versions of me. Even Dad was Ray or Raymond or Mr. Cariou to other people, and on the diplomas in his office he was Raymondum Geraldum Cariouum. That was the funniest name of all. Mom was Melba or Mrs. Cariou, and to our English friends she was Melber. How could we be so many different things? It seemed that names were the briefest, most cryptic kind of stories, and that it would take a lifetime to puzzle out their plots and settings and characters.

Sometimes Dad told us our stories in the living room, or the backyard, or in the car as we drove to Canwood or Leonard's Ranch or the cabin, but the ones we counted on were the bedtime variety. Bedtime was in fact renamed storytime, in a fully successful attempt to quell our rebellions against the early hour (eight-thirty) of our appointed slumbers. For storytime we were willing to go to bed any time after supper.

Glenn and I shared a bedroom, and Dad would come in once we had said our prayers, or claimed to, and we would all climb into one tiny, quivering, plastic-sheeted bed. We lay on our backs, Glenn and I nestling under each of Dad's arms, resting our heads on his shoulders. When Michelle was old enough she joined in too, the three of us Lilliputians on Dad's Gulliverian body. We looked up at the stippled ceiling with its tiny winking sparkles that glimmered like distant stars. Streetlight came in through the window, seeping past the navy blue curtains. In winter the aquamarine of our outside Christmas lights illumined the frost patterns on the glass. Sometimes I would scrape my initials in that frost at night and would wake up the next morning to find the letters transmogrified by cold into curlicued rococo fonts like the ones at the beginnings of fairy tales.

"Okay. Where was I?" Dad would say, and we'd have to remind him, because each night's story was somehow connected to the previous one and there could be no such thing as starting anew.

Sometimes he told us about where *he* was from, the town of Ituna in the southern part of Saskatchewan, where we had never been. He had grown up on a farm near Ituna with his mother and fourteen siblings. His dad had died when he was six or seven but he didn't tell us about that. Instead he described the funny characters in the town and the trouble that he and his brothers got into. There was the story of Handlebar Harry, the Ituna barber who had fallen asleep in his barber's chair one afternoon and awakened to find— eeyike!—one half of his handlebar moustache lying on the floor like a turd. (Dad always punctuated his tales with "eeyaws!" or "eeyikes!" at the many turning points of his plots.) There was the story of Jimmy Kobialchuk the bully, taunting Dad and Uncle Leo from the other side of a fence, watching them through a knothole in the wood. Uncle Leo put a rock in his slingshot and whap! shot Jimmy right through the knothole, gave him a black eye.

There were stories about hunting gophers, snaring fish, grabbing partridges out of trees. He told us about the egg collection he and Uncle Charlie had: dozens of bird eggs, raided from the nests of sparrows, magpies, hawks, several species of duck, two kinds of geese, and a great horned owl, which had cost Uncle Charlie some scars. Dad described the process of "blowing" the eggs to keep them from spoiling: they poked a needle hole in each end, then put the eggs up to their lips and blew the insides out the far end, as if playing some mucousy musical instrument. They kept the eggs in a straw-lined box, a kind of condominium nest, and they brought them out for solemn viewings whenever the neighbourhood kids asked. But their local fame as egg collectors was short-lived. At some offence they had given, Uncle Vic raided their collection and played pool with the eggs on the floor of the barn.

Dad also told many stories about Meadow Lake and points north: legends of trappers who sewed themselves into their long underwear for the whole winter; a farmer who hid his money in an old threshing machine; a commercial fisherman who drove so fast on the corduroy roads that every last one of his frozen fish bounced out the back of his truck. We learned about mythical northerners named Rosie Belly and Nelson Cannapotatoes and Banjo Ratt. We heard tales of the glorious fishing and hunting in the early days, as told to Dad by a trapper named Babe Stonehocker, whom we met a few years later when he hitched a ride with us down to Saskatoon. (I remember being shocked to discover that he was real, and that his favourite drink was cream soda.)

There were also more fanciful animal tales, about foxes, rabbits, and Chippy the chipmunk, who lived in the trees behind our cabin at the lake. My favourites were the ones about Simpleton Simon Sasquatch, who was brought back by popular demand night after night. The first instalment of the Simpleton Saga began something like this:

"Simpleton Simon Sasquatch lived alone as most Sasquatches do. But he wasn't like most Sasquatches, because he didn't enjoy it, being by himself. And from the beginning, even when he was just a little Squatch (that's what they called baby Sasquatches), he was different in another way too: he liked people. Bald-faces is what they were called. And Simpleton Simon liked them. He didn't want to stay hidden in the caves, to sleep in the tallest treetops, to run bounding down the canyon walls as soon as a bald-face came walking or driving or flying along. 'Why do we have to hide?' he asked his parents, and they answered, 'Why do we have to eat? Why do we breathe? Why do we have to be born, and get old, and die?' And for his trouble, he earned the name Simpleton, because they thought only a fool would ask such a question.

"Simpleton Simon left home when he grew up, and wandered in search of a friend. He lived in the mountains, but he had to walk far, far away from them to find a place that looked friendly. Most times, when he tried to introduce himself to bald-faces, they got out their cameras or their guns. None of them reached out to shake his hand. So he kept wandering, down past the foothills, across the prairie, and even past the edge of a big smoky city. After that he went further north, because he didn't like the smell of the smoke. In the north he liked the trees and the birds and especially the berries. He lived on berries, and loved blueberries the best.

"After crossing fields and swamps and rivers and highways, Simpleton Simon came to a town at the edge of a lake. It was not a grand or famous town, but the people smiled to each other as he watched them from a distance, and the northern lights dazzled him night after night, and everywhere the berries hung from the plants like grapes.

"'I like the taste of this place,' said Simpleton Simon, munching on a dewberry. 'I think I'll call it home.'"

I don't remember all of Dad's stories, but what remains in my memory is the magic of lying there in the dark and witnessing the tale as it came into being, out of nothing, at the very moment we heard it. No two were ever the same, even when we asked for repeat performances. Anything could—and did— happen, while Handlebar Harry reached up to feel the stump of his former moustache, while Simpleton Simon Sasquatch fell into the bread-dough machinery at the Meadow Lake Bakery and had to swim the Labrea Dough-Pits, while Uncle Vic cued up an empty great horned owl egg and knocked it to smithereens. I drifted to sleep with Dad's stories parading in my head, and I often dreamed about them too.

Very early, I decided these tales needed to be preserved. I guess even then I understood that Dad wouldn't always be around to tell them for us. Sometimes Glenn and Michelle and I retold them to each other, or acted them out, or even shared them with the neighbour boys, Roger and Stephen. But these performances, too, disappeared as soon as the words were spoken, and I worried. I didn't have Dad's instinctive trust in the resilience of the story as it passes from mouth to memory and on to other people like a benevolent bacterium, always alive and giving life.

This is how I came to be a writer before I could read. Many evenings I sat on the couch with a Giant scribbler on my knees, serious as a stenographer, inscribing row after row of curlicues, which represented the collected stories of Simpleton Simon Sasquatch and Rosie Belly and all my aunts and uncles.

And now Dad is gone, and I'm still scribbling. Not only to preserve but also to understand those stories and the people and places that inspired them. And to continue on in Dad's tradition, turning life into stories and stories into life. Because if they are where I come from, then maybe they can tell me something about where I belong.

These days I am more concerned than ever about belonging, because I know how fragile it is. There is a crisis of belonging in the world. We are all restless; we are on the move. It is the age of migration and diaspora, the age of commuting, and many of us feel the strain of the contemporary mania for being everywhere at once. But I don't think we need to stay in one place all our lives in order to reconnect with our environments. We need instead to re-examine our stories, to discover a more fluid kind of belonging, one that melds memory and voice and sensation into the complex geometry of our lives.

That's what I have tried to do in this book. It is a story of belonging, an account of my myriad connections to the place I come from and the family that brought me there. Meadow Lake might be an insignificant place in the eyes of the larger world, but it has been crucially important to me, and I want to explore that personal importance. I suspect that most people have a Meadow Lake of their own, a place they can't let go of. They need not have been born in that place, or still live there now, but somehow it has taken hold of them and shaped them so irrevocably that they can't imagine who they would be without it. That's how it is for me. I have lived away from Meadow Lake for almost half my life, and I will probably never live there again, yet it is still unquestionably the place I mean when I say "home."

Sometimes this attachment puzzles me. What is the nature of my connection to this place? Why can't I just get on with the business of adopting a new home wherever I happen to live? Why is my imagination so crowded with the citizens and skies and teeming forests of Meadow Lake?

Whenever I think about belonging—to a community, a place, a family, an association—I return to that ubiquitous childhood question: Where do I come from? It has turned out to be one of the most difficult and necessary questions for me, not because origins provide the answers but because origins must be questioned deeply and continually if we are to be at home in the world in a meaningful way. The closer we look at our stories of origin, the more likely we are to find other and sometimes contradictory stories beneath them. And it can be a lifelong task, to learn the many histories of the place and the family you come from. What traditions, what secrets, what disasters, what subterfuges and wars and inventions and loves were necessary for me to become the person I am? And am I somehow responsible for these origins? What sway do they hold over me?

As I have remembered and questioned and imagined the stories of my home, I have learned many things about it. I learned that a rambunctious boy like my schoolmate Clayton Matchee could grow up into a soldier, and that a soldier from Meadow Lake could learn to hate so perfectly that he could be involved in a torture and murder that shocked the world. I discovered that there had been secrets in my family for two generations, and that I wasn't quite who I thought I was. I learned that my own happiness didn't make me innocent. I learned that when people die they leave a space in the world, and that long afterward the living can press their bodies against that space, and listen.

Coming through tall red-top grass near Meadow Lake, 1909.
(FRANK CREAN PHOTO)

PLACE NAMES

I am from a place called Meadow Lake, Saskatchewan.

I practised that story to myself, held it ready for anyone who might ask. I was three or four. I knew that as long as I could remember those words, I would never be lost. No matter where I was, I could just tell a policeman "I'm from Meadow Lake," and he would take me home.

Or so I told myself. I was never entirely convinced, though, because for one thing, I didn't really know what Meadow Lake was. It had more identities than I did, more even than Raymondum Geraldum. Sometimes it was "M.L." or "Meadow" or "Meddle Ache," or just "town." The Chamber of Commerce called it "Gateway to Pure Air and Water," but I had heard others call it "Mudow Lake" and "Indianville" and simply "this hole." Then there was the problem of the many neighbourhoods: Snob Hill, Little Chicago, the two trailer parks, the stampede grounds, Railway Avenue. All of these were Meadow Lake, but not all of them were home.

I learned years later that Meadow Lake had been given many other names in previous generations. In the late nineteenth and early twentieth centuries, the Metis inhabitants called it Lac des Prairies, or sometimes Lac de Prairie. In 1909, a rough-and-tumble surveyor named Frank Crean called the region "Canada's Fertile Northland" and "the New Northwest" in the two government-sponsored pamphlets he wrote to encourage settlement in the area. In the second of these he declared that Meadow Lake contained "some of the very finest farm land in Canada," and he predicted that the place would realize its magnificent potential as soon as an influx of farmers arrived. More than a century earlier, fur trader Peter Fiddler had given the place a more forbidding name, calling it Barren Grounds Lake. He named his trading post Bolsover House, after his birthplace in England. And long before and since all these names, the Cree people have called it Pasqua Shaghigan, or in the new orthography Paskwâw Sâkâhikan, which means prairie lake.

But Meadow Lake is not located in the region known as the Prairies, even though it's in Saskatchewan. This is a Saskatchewan that doesn't exist in the popular imagination: a treed Saskatchewan, of rock and water and muskeg and— wherever these last three are not found—fertile soil. The northern half of the province is cloaked in boreal forest, which is also somewhat euphemistically called the parkland (timberland might be more accurate, given the importance of forestry in the area). Meadow Lake is less than sixty miles from the transition between parkland and prairie, but still it is firmly ensconced in the geography and the ethos of the north. I'm certain, for example, that if it was in the south it would have had different names. It could only be called Meadow Lake or Lac des Prairies or Paskwâw Sâkâhikan in a region where prairie was an anomaly. In the south, *all* lakes are surrounded by prairie, but in the north the vast majority of them are treed right to the shoreline. In this context, the meadow of Meadow Lake was what made the place unique, what made it nameable.

When I was growing up I didn't think much about either the meadow or the lake. The meadow had disappeared long before I was born, and the lake was frankly unattractive, at least from the point of view of sightseers, swimmers, and anglers. Maybe in another place, farther south, the town would have become accustomed to its namesake and would eventually have accepted it, but here there are dozens of gorgeous, pristine lakes within an hour's drive of the community. When the townspeople talk about going "up to the lake," they always mean some other lake, clearer and deeper and more picturesque than the one that neighbours the town and shares its name. Few people ever fish there, except occasionally on the backwater that extends past the golf course and eventually disappears in the fields south of our farm.

I, having been a fanatic angler from my earliest days, was one of those few. I used to ride out to the backwater on my bike, along with my friends Roger and Kenten, with our fishing rods sticking out across our handlebars, and we would fish for whatever slimy monsters the backwater would bequeath us. All it held was dullard warmwater pike, which fought like a rubber boot, as Dad used to say. I remember once catching a little pike while standing on the narrow bridge that crossed the backwater just outside of town. The fish bit the hook and then didn't move at all. Not knowing if I could scramble down the bank to land it, I just kept reeling, and the fish came straight up out of the water like a dredged corpse. It was utterly stationary, dangling down from my Len Thompson spoon with a sluggish inertia that was indeed remarkably like a rubber boot full of water. I was so unnerved by its stillness and its ghastly grey colour that I stopped cranking when it was five or six feet out of the water. We all stared at it for several seconds, without anyone offering me the customary congratulations. Then suddenly the pike convulsed, a Frankensteinian shudder that was just strong enough to dislodge it from the hook. It splatted down on the muddy water and was gone. This was the only time I have been thankful to lose a fish.

I've been told that the eponymous meadow was a large natural clearing that began at the edge of the lake, but I don't know exactly where it was because its boundaries were obliterated many years ago when the surrounding forest was logged. I suppose that for the first homesteaders, in the early decades of the twentieth century, the attraction of this location was not the lake but the meadow, which would have been a windfall to any ranchers searching for grazing land, or any farmers seeking to clear their requisite ten acres in such a densely forested area. Certainly they used it intensively, and because of that there are few vestiges of the meadow left. It was seeded with wheat or barley or alfalfa, or else turned into pasture. The townsite itself was probably once meadow, as was the golf course. Some of the municipal pastureland south of town offers the closest approximation of the land's earlier state, but even that has been altered by the grazing habits of the legions of cattle that have summered there.

When I try to picture the meadow now, it's like imagining an entirely different place, a place I have never been.

Based on the photos taken by Frank Crean's surveying expedition in 1909, I know it was a tall-grass prairie, a rare spot in this northern forest where sunlight could penetrate nearly to the ground. In summer it would have hosted big bluestem grasses and daisies and prairie lilies, and perhaps delicate lady's slippers. It would have been populated at times by woodland caribou, elk, moose, white-tailed deer, and dozens of smaller animals and birds. The Cree people would have hunted along the perimeter of the meadow, and they would have gathered berries and roots there.

Not all of this has been lost. Native people still hunt in the area and gather their traditional foods, though many of them have also taken jobs in town or at the sawmill to support themselves. Almost all the plants and animals that once lived here can still be found in the area, and some of them, such as the deer, are probably faring better now than they did before the farmers came and planted high-yield crops for them to eat. But everything has had to adapt to the changes that deforestation, cultivation, fencing, and road building brought along with them. Many of the species that thrived before are now struggling. Recognizing this is enough to make me lament the coming of the farmers and foresters and community builders who pushed so many things out of the way in order to make a settlement. But this thought puts me in an uncomfortable position. If those people hadn't come and hadn't brought those changes, then I could never have called this place home.

The town itself is clustered at the edge of a bog about a mile from the western shore of the lake. For anyone who doesn't think of it as home, Meadow Lake might be thought to have few attractions, other than its proximity to the grandeur of the northern boreal forest. It is a sleepy town, a violent town, a town with secrets, a town of simple beauty and brazen ugliness. It resonates with contradictions, like many communities. The most impressive architectural monument is not the library or the town hall or any of the churches; it's the liquor store—a great slanting postmodern behemoth that seems to be leaning on the pool hall to the south of it, as if the building itself is drunk. Some of the older stores on Main Street still have the false fronts popular in frontier architecture and Hollywood westerns. The town has only one set of traffic lights, much derided by our city cousins when they came to visit. *Oooooeeeee, we're going through THE light. . . . Hey, is it true they switch it off on Sundays? Is that so the little man inside can go to church?*

Most of the traffic is half-ton trucks, usually with quads or snowmobiles in the back for ballast. In the evenings, the teenagers prowl up and down Main Street in their fathers' F-150s and Rams and Silverados, leaning out the windows at the traffic light to ask each other, "Where's the party?" There's not much else to do, some say, but that really isn't true. There is the seasonal cycle of outdoor activities: fishing, golf, hunting, curling; fishing, golf, hunting, curling. You could calibrate a calendar on the basis of the various opening days and closing days, the tournaments, the bonspiels. For those with different tastes there is also hockey, snowmobiling, ice fishing, water-skiing, and hot-tubbing. The town has a movie theatre and a swimming pool and a bowling alley. And there is always bingo. Bingo is undoubtedly the most popular leisure activity

in the district, except for driving. This is why the biggest jackpot prizes are always brand-new trucks.

There isn't much time for leisure in Meadow Lake,
though. If you're not mending your own fence, fixing your
own car, building your own deck, or roofing your own house
after work, you are expected to be helping someone else with
their projects. People are proud of their physical work, their
ability to take care of things on their own. It is more hon-
ourable to do the work yourself than to hire someone.
Farmers, mechanics, truck drivers, lumberjacks, and carpenters are the model citizens in Meadow Lake, even if they are
not the best paid. The bosses and the businesspeople are tolerated, but they are often sheepish about their authority, their
lack of visible productivity. Sometimes they try to compen-
sate by building their own houses or learning to pilot float
planes or going hunting for two months every fall.

The winters in Meadow Lake are longer than all the
other seasons put together, and the scant, glorious summers
are plagued with insects. Floods, fires, blizzards, hailstorms,
and tornadoes seem always imminent. On the coldest winter
days, you risk your life by simply driving out of town. But the
place is also undeniably beautiful. The landscape has the stillness and intimacy of the forest, yet somehow it also cradles
the vast and luminous prairie sky. You only have to walk
among the trees or look up at the sky to understand why
people live there.

Between the north shore of the lake and the eastern edge
of town is the Flying Dust Cree Nation, which is marked
by a few large administrative buildings and a scattering of

multicoloured but identically shaped houses along the high-way. It has existed since 1878, when Chief Kopahawakemim and his hastily assembled band signed Treaty No. 6, and for a long time it was known officially as Reserve 105 or Meadow Lake Indian Reserve. Before the treaty agents came, it must have seemed absurd to the Crees that the land could be named and divided and apportioned simply by making cryptic marks on a piece of paper. But since the treaty, the people of Flying Dust have had to become accustomed to the dictates of that paper: the ways it has kept them separate and has controlled their relationship to the land.

To me the Flying Dust Nation was simply known as the reserve. I hardly ever went out there, except to drive through it on our way to go fishing at Leonard's Ranch or skiing in the St. Cyr Hills or, in later years, to inspect the calves in our pasture. Every time we drove past, I scanned the yards and road allowances and fields, hoping to see the dust that the place was named for. I imagined a whirlwind shimmying across the landscape, sweeping up chip bags and dried leaves along with the column of dust. But I never saw anything like that on the reserve, and I was always disappointed that it didn't live up to its name. Turns out I was looking for the wrong thing. Years later I learned that Flying Dust was named after a person rather than any attribute of the place. Chief Kopahawakemim's name means "where the dust flies up."

The reserve didn't feel like a destination to me, partly because it was so close to town. It also felt somehow off-limits, even though I went to school with kids from there, and the people of Flying Dust were very much a part of everyday life in Meadow Lake. The few times we did stop there—to watch a baseball game with Uncle Vic, or to get gas at the service station—I felt conspicuous, vulnerable. Like a trespasser. For some reason I was more comfortable in other reserves farther north, which we sometimes visited on our fishing trips or berry-picking expeditions, or when we just went "out for a drive," as Mom and Dad so often liked to do. We went to the reserve at Canoe Lake for fishing, to the one at Waterhen Lake for cabin supplies and sometimes for church services, and occasionally to the Metis communities in Green Lake and Beauval for more fishing. Mom worked for a while as a public health nurse in various Native communities, at the Joseph Bighead Reserve and the Loon Lake Reserve.

There are ten First Nations in the Meadow Lake area, of Cree and Dene people, and there are numerous settlements of Metis and Non-Status indigenous people. Some of these reserves and settlements are relatively prosperous—like the Flying Dust Nation—and others are less so. But one thing is certain: all of them are growing, even though many of the young people have been leaving for the cities in recent years. If anyone were to examine the population of aboriginal people in the area and compare it with the population of settlers, it is possible that the Natives would outnumber the whites.

The district is far from being a utopia of racial harmonization. There has always been a certain amount of tension between the settlers and the indigenous people in Meadow Lake, and I don't think the town is at all unusual in this. There are land claims of various kinds, and there have been blockades, and there have been outbreaks of violence. Most of the time the tension just simmers, fuelled by racism and inequality and long-held grudges. In some parts of North

America, the turmoil and the violence that accompanied settlement occurred a long time ago, but in Meadow Lake, the major wave of settlement happened at the edge of living memory—close enough in time that the wounds are still raw.

Many settlers came to Meadow Lake in an attempt to escape the upheavals of large-scale history: wars, dislocations, droughts, famines. Someone once told me about an elderly couple who chose to come to Meadow Lake from Poland because they thought it must be the safest place in the world. I never met this couple, and they may not even have existed —they might have been a figment of Meadow Lake's more utopian ideas of itself. Nevertheless, they made a good point about the place. Wars have been unlikely in northern Saskatchewan, at least since 1885, and earthquakes are virtually impossible, and drought is much less of a threat in Meadow Lake than in the arid southern parts of the province. The people have a tradition of looking out for each other, too: the Saskatchewan government was the first in North America to introduce universal health care. If someone was looking for a place to retire from the ills of modernity, Meadow Lake might seem like an ideal location.

Certainly, many immigrants found their way to the area, whether or not they held such idealistic hopes for it as the legendary Polish couple. There is a large community of Ukrainian people in the district, most of them farmers, and all of them proud of their heritage. Ukrainian weddings and New Year's celebrations are famous for their arrays of food, dancing, and elaborate traditional costumes. There are some Irish families, some Scottish, some French, and a few Scandinavians, most of whom work in the forest. Two

Chinese families operate restaurants, as in many prairie towns. More recently there have been South African immigrants, all of them white, and most of them doctors. One of these couples told me that they had left everything behind—a beautiful house, two cars, a dog—to escape the escalating violence in their city. To them, a few months after their arrival, Meadow Lake was an oasis.

Even looking at this minuscule sample of the immigrant populace, I get the impression that people are flowing like some volatile liquid over the globe, seeking a place to cling onto, a place to belong. A few of them have found that here. They have learned their own ways of coming to terms with the place, making it into a home, even if they have other faraway homes too. Those who love the place most are usually the ones who love the outdoors—hunting, fishing, canoeing, skiing. I have sat many times on riverbanks with people from almost every corner of the world, all of us enjoying the fresh though mosquito-ridden air, all of us hoping to catch a pickerel. How strange that we should all end up in such a place, festooned with the bizarre implements of angling—rod, tackle box, beer can, ball cap, sunflower seeds, styrofoam cup full of leeches—each grinning with the knowledge that there is no better place and no better time than right here and right now.

Many other people choose not to live in Meadow Lake, either because they can't find opportunity there or because they don't feel they can make it a home. For those who grow up there, leaving town is often a burning ambition. Most of the young people still leave after high school, with varying degrees of regret and elation. Other people come to town for a few years and then move on. Our friends the Chungs came from Vietnam and lived in Meadow Lake for seven or eight years before moving to Toronto. I think they still have fond memories of our town, but they had been urban people before, and they felt a need for a larger Vietnamese community.

And even for those of us who call Meadow Lake home, it is not always possible to stay there. Jobs and loves and plain old restlessness can take people away, and can make it very difficult to return. I know this from experience. But still I like to think it's possible to retain that attachment from a distance, to take a place with you when you leave. Stories, after all, are portable.

Cree men near Waterhen Lake, 1909.
(FRANK CREAN PHOTO)

THE TELLING

It didn't take me long to realize that Meadow Lake was just like my family: everyone talking, in unison or at cross purposes, arguing about what had happened or what was going to happen. As in any small town, gossip was the fabric of the community. We gossiped each other into being. There were rumours of cancer (always accompanied by grim and invented prognoses); accusations of lechery, alcoholism, incompetence, and embezzlement; speculations about who would soon run off with the delivery man, who was "slapping around" his wife, and who was burglarizing the Lux Theatre every second Saturday night. There were many accounts of accidental deaths, by drowning, by fire, by agricultural mishap and industrial accident. One local boy had even died of rabies after being bitten by an infected bat. My friend Jimmy was the first to tell me, though it had happened at least a decade before.

"A kid over by Dom Bosco, he died of a bat bite."

"Ch!"

"Uh-huh. He come down to his room at bedtime and there it was swooping over his bed like that and he tried to catch it in his dad's fishing net but it bit him in the hand like a snake with two little tooth marks and he didn't tell anybody 'cause he didn't want sevenneedlesinthestomach that's what they do if a bat bites you you know and the needles are six inches long but still if you ask me it's bettern what happened to him 'cause he growled and went crazy and wouldn't take a bath and then his brain swole up and started coming out his mouth and he died like that choking on his own brain and it was only in the funeral parlour when they saw the fangprints on his hand that they knew what'd happened."

"No way."

"Yes way. Ask my mom."

Stupid deaths and dismemberments were common themes in our municipal folklore. In addition to the bat-bite boy, there was the apocryphal girl who had drowned in a puddle of water, the various snowmobile-and-barbed-wire-fence decapitations, the foolish electrocutions of yesteryear.

"Such a shame," people would say.

But also: "Fuckin' idyit."

To be scorned and mourned at once was the pinnacle of notoriety. One inventive teenager decided to stick a .22 bullet into the glowing coils of a car's cigarette lighter, just to see what would happen. All he lost was the tip of his index finger, but his recklessness earned him an almost enviable local immortality.

Meadow Lake was also the world capital of fish stories, the vast majority of which were lies. But they weren't just your run-of-the-mill arm-stretchers—they were interesting lies; lies with panache. The kids at our swimming lessons told a story about a skin diver who had been attacked by a huge northern pike just down from the public beach. He had fired a speargun at the monster, but the spear had bounced harmlessly off its prehistoric skull. Another time, outside the filleting shack at Canoe Lake, an old man told me about the Cree ladies who could fillet a pickerel so fast that when they tossed the skeleton back in the water it would swim away.

"Sometimes they keep bitin' for a few minutes," he said, "and you have to throw 'em back twice."

When I was nine or ten, my farm friends Marlon and Wade told me they used to *shoot* fish, in the crik that flowed through their west quarter, standing on an overhanging log with .22s aimed down between their feet, firing into their own reflections. There was never any question that they were telling the truth, because they told me with such uncharacteristic offhandedness.

"Shot four suckers an' a slough shark after school. Fed 'em to the pigs."

I was never sure what to make of Marlon and Wade. They were incontrovertible evidence of the vast and mysterious divide between farm kids and town kids. Even their vocabulary was different. They said crik instead of creek, and dinner instead of lunch, and when a sow had her babies they said "she pigged." They uttered threats about each other's "coils" ("You don't shut the fuck up I'll boot ya square in the coil"), and they asked if I knew how to "drive truck." Both of *them* drove truck, and drove tractor, and sometimes even drove combine. They also knew how to weld, and how to skin a coyote (I was puzzled they didn't say "skin coyote"), and they could grab the electric fence for three seconds at a time without crying. It was entirely possible that they would fearlessly blast away at the calm surface of the crik until the bottom was coated with lead.

Much as I was impressed by Marlon and Wade, I also believed they were prime candidates for stupid death. I had been told that water was the most dangerous thing you could shoot at, and that no one in their right mind would do it. Roger's older brother Philip, who had taken Hunter Safety, told us that a bullet could skip like a stone, and you never knew where it would end up. He told us about a man who went deer hunting near Midnight Lake while his wife was driving along the highway on the far side. This hunter took a practice shot at the water with his brand-new thirty-aught-six, and the bullet ricocheted off the surface at the perfect angle to fly across the lake, smash through the driver's window, and imbed itself in his wife's neck.

I imagined Marlon and Wade shooting each other at the exact same moment, their bullets glancing off the treacherous crik and into their respective hearts, the lucky fish scattering upstream, laughing their bubbly fish laughter as the brothers tumbled into the mucky water, still clutching their guns. While this scenario was not altogether unattractive, I didn't want to be responsible for their martyrdom. So I told on them.

The idea had occurred to me more than once, but the opportunity didn't present itself until one sunny Saturday afternoon in October, when Dad and I were visiting their farm. I left Marlon and Wade throwing jackknives at each other behind the machine shed, and I found their dad standing by a corral with my dad and a group of other men, inspecting a black bull with droopy horns. Mr. Lajeunesse was an immense man with fingers as thick as hammer handles, and I remembered him once picking up a hay bale in each hand and standing there in the field as if they were empty lunch buckets. I had no doubt that he could lift that Aberdeen Angus bull over his head and shot-put it across the corral. His strength was almost absurd, which I suppose was why I didn't find him frightening. That and his skill at bull-shitting. He was more likely to talk your ear off than tear you limb from limb.

"Mr. Lajeunesssssse . . .," I said, glancing back to be sure the brothers were still out of earshot. "Marlon 'n' Wade said they were shootin' fish in the cri—ik."

He gave me a look. "Yeah . . .? I taught 'em that."

Some of the men chuckled, and my dad joined in for a second, though there was a look of uncertainty, of mixed allegiances, in his eyes.

"But the bullets, you never know where, I heard there was a guy—"

"Naaaaah," he said. "It's okay, long's you shoot straight down. That's the thing. I always used to shoot water—hell, we shot ice too. We shot hundreds a big jacks through the ice when I was a kid at Sled Lake. Them jacks, they'd come in real shallow in the fall, I dunno why—for warmth maybe. And when the ice was an inch thick we could still see 'em swimming under there, me and my brothers. So we took a .22 and an axe and we went out there, boy, and that ice was cracking and squealing and bouncing whenever you took a step, and the bubbles shaking underneath. And we hunted. Hunted for fish.

"We'd sneak right up on them damn big jacks and shoot 'em in the top of the head, right through the ice and the whole bit. Bingo. Toughest thing was knowing where to dig the hole, 'cause them damn fish would shimmy like this once they were shot"—here Mr. Lajeunesse attempted something like the jitterbug, with a look of piscine desperation on his huge red face— "and they'd shimmy like that for a while and then stop, and one of my brothers would start chopping the hole to get them out. And then them buggers would shimmy a little more. Chop. Wiggle. Chop. Wiggle. Noise must've scared 'em, though I dunno what they had to be scared about, seeing as how they were already dead. Not like anything worse is gonna happen, eh? But they were nervous fish, I guess. Nervous dead fish.

"And sometimes they wiggled out over deep water, but we always followed 'em, moving quick on that springy ice, eh, hardly letting your feet touch down, like you're walking hot coals or that. Never did fall in. That Gerald, though, he lost an axe once—chop, chop, sploosh—and did *he* catch hell when we got home, believe you me, boy.

"But anyways. Water and ice're perfectly safe to shoot, long as you're not stupid about it. Or unlucky."

The men laughed again, and a few of them launched into fragmentary reminiscences of crazy tricks with guns and blasting caps and dynamite. I stopped listening. By this time I had forgotten my traitorous designs on Marlon and Wade, and I was planning a visit to Philip's place, where I would tell him the error of his ways.

But in the jeep on our way back home, Dad told me that it *was,* actually, dangerous as hell to shoot at water, and he'd better not catch me trying it when I was finally allowed to shoot a gun.

"Why?" I asked. "Who'm I supposed to believe?"

"You believe whoever pays for your groceries," he said.

There were poaching stories in Meadow Lake too, in which the game wardens (called the D.N.R.) were always the bumbling villains. And moonshine stories, with jocular references to exploding stills and epidemics of blindness and spectacular car crashes like on *Dukes of Hazzard*. But never any mention of marijuana operations BECAUSE DRUGS WERE WRONG AND ONLY FOR DEPRAVED CITY CRIMINALS AND HIPPIE COMMUNISTS, neither of whom were welcome in town.

There were taunts and rumours about Makwa Jane, a toothless Native prostitute who allegedly haunted the Main Street bars. *She's comin' for you, boy. Gonna get ya by the short 'n' curlies. She knows ya want 'er.*

There were many other Indian stories. Tubby Evanishen told me if the Indians ever caught you they'd bury you up to your neck and pin your eyelids wide open with safety pins till the sun fried your eyes like eggs.

I passed this story on to my friend Jimmy.

"*I'm* part Cree," he said.

"Oh."

You could never be sure who was an Indian.

There were stories about the fights in the bars and at the annual stampede dances, which seemed to be as much a part of the entertainment as the local country bands were. At one stampede dance, Uncle Leo and Uncle Charlie had tried to break up a fight and had ended up slugging it out with the rest of them. Another time, a carload of young punks were taunting Mr. Lajeunesse in the arena parking lot from the safety of their Trans Am, shouting threats and insults through a one-inch opening in the driver's window. He was patient with them, considering that drunk young men were always provoking him, trying to impress each other with their recklessness. He ignored them for quite a while, trying to recount a convoluted moose-hunting story to the assembled rye-and-Coke-sipping men. But the boys kept interrupting. *Hey. Fats. What's yer problem, don't ya got ears?* Gunning the engine for punctuation. Finally, at a crucial moment in his story, Mr. Lajeunesse stepped casually up to the Trans Am, wedged his fingers inside the window, and yanked the glass right out of the door.

"Ya better go get this fixed," he said, handing it back to the speechless driver.

Or so I was told.

Everyone told everyone so many things.

Mr. Pape, the groundskeeper at the golf course, told me and Leonard to *stay* the *hell* off the *god*damn *tops* of the *christ's* sake *hills* when the *sky's* all *shit*tin' down *hail* and *light*ning like that, or yer *balls* 'll be *fried* 'n' *froze* at *once.*

Fabian Lehoux told me his method for getting a girl-friend: "Whatcha do, ya buy 'er a fur coat 'n' that, 'n' 'en she'll show ya 'er pussy."

I told everyone, "I swear to god I seen a bass this—THIS!—big, under the boat launch dock at Jeannette Lake."

Jimmy told me his friend Ricky Gulack could bend metal bars with his bare hands—and he *could*, too. I saw it with my own eyes. Ricky sat on his mom's front step and stomped a cowboy boot into the middle of a stolen copper tube, and then leaned back and yanked with his quivering shoulders as if to launch a crossbow bolt over the neighbouring rooftops. He made the *Six Million Dollar Man* noise—*Da* na na na na na na, *Da* na na na na na na na—as the bar slowly crumpled into a V.

Sister Madeleine told our catechism class that the Blessed Virgin once appeared to Saint Simon Stock and gave him a small cloth necklace and promised him, "Whosoever Weareth This Brown Scapular Shall Not Suffer Eternal Fire." Then I won the prayer memorization contest with a perfect Hail Mary, two-thirds of a Glory Be, and a verse of the Apostles' Creed. The prize was a scapular necklace of my very own: a free ticket out of hell, a licence to sin. For months I carried it in my pocket, just in case.

The ladies I overheard at the Co-op lunch counter told each other about something I couldn't figure out.

"So I guess that Johnson girl went'n got herself in—"

"*Really.*"

"Arla at the clinic says."

"Who's the—?"

"Well she won't *tell* now, will she."

"Could be any a the hockey players, I'd say."

Oh, there was no end to the telling.

Sometimes there were even stories from books, though they were slightly less compelling than the ones I heard around me every day. Still, I was dedicated to them. I attended Story Hour every week in Meadow Lake's overcrowded one-room library. The building was so small that it had no bathroom. There was only a dark and musty utility room behind the checkout desk, which was crammed with janitorial supplies, old books, binding glue, and brightly coloured rolls of tape. Just inside the door, four feet off the ground, was a sink. If you had to pee, the only option was to climb up the wobbly stepladder braced against the sink, balance there while undoing your pants, and then aim down into the tiny porcelain bowl. I remember how the librarian, Mrs. Gorst, had explained this arrangement to me the first time—with unwavering dignity, as if it was perfectly normal to climb a ladder before urinating. I asked her if the girls had to do this too, but she ignored me. She simply stepped outside and pulled the door shut behind her, leaving me to my target practice.

The worst thing was that the door had no lock. I was sure it would swing wide open and the whole Story Hour crowd would see me standing up there on that shaky pedestal in all my glory. Just the thought that this could happen was a cause of great anxiety and less-than-perfect aim.

Let it never be said that I haven't suffered for the love of stories. Unfortunately the trauma of the sink is so strong in my mind that I don't recall the stories very well. There was one about a skunk, I think, and one about elephants—probably Babar. What I do remember is the calm, soothing sound of Mrs. Gorst's voice and the swooping movements of her eyebrows when she read the dialogue. I was enthralled. I sat there in the late-afternoon light, my feet dangling from the wooden chair, oblivious to the other kids around me. For this, even the indignity of the ladder was worth it.

But even though I was deluged with stories, there were many more that I didn't hear or didn't understand. I wondered what the Native people were saying to each other when they gathered on the sidewalks of Main Street, teasing and cajoling in their soft syllables of Cree. "Ihhh!" they would say, or "Ch!" And then they would cup their mouths around that language and something unknown would come out. I knew only four words of Cree: *tâpwe, makikway, tansi,* and *nîstâw.* Jimmy had taught them to me, along with a few curses of dubious authenticity. I listened for these recognizable fragments, and sometimes I thought I heard them. Occasionally the speakers would even break into phrases of English, spiced by that distinctive accent. But even when I knew the words, I couldn't piece together the stories.

It was the same with the Ukrainian voices, the Low German of the Hutterites, the Cantonese in our two Chinese restaurants, and even the French, though Grandma Laliberte spoke French too, and my dad appeared to understand it. Also the Jehovah's Witnesses, though of course they did speak English, and in fact they broadcast their messages on every doorstep in town. Still they mystified me. "We have our own religion, thanks," Mom would tell them at the door, and they would move along to our neighbours without even leaving a pamphlet. I wondered what they did in their windowless Kingdom Hall, what kind of prayers they said. They were impossibly esoteric to me, a secret society. And yet they were out evangelizing in the streets.

I never spoke to the black man who worked in the pool hall, though I was fascinated with his Afro and his large, quizzical eyes. His laugh shook him like a marionette, and everyone in the place—even the toughest toughs—couldn't stop themselves from smiling when they heard it. He reminded me of a TV star because television was the only other place I had seen a black man. I watched him from the row of pinball machines, wondering how he had got to Meadow Lake and why he stayed there. I didn't have the nerve to ask him.

There were also the old, the sick, and the handicapped, who were kept from the commerce of the town by their debilitations. Shut-ins, Mom called them. That label was terrifying in its finality. It sounded like a door closing. *Shut-in.* I had never seen a shut-in, naturally, though Mom went to visit them sometimes, bringing meals on wheels or medications. I imagined they lived in tiny, boarded-up houses, imprisoned by their infirmities, ignored by the rest of the world. Quarantined. Their silences resonated against the tumult and cacophony of the town. To me, it seemed they had prematurely become ghosts.

But I knew that even the people I *did* hear and did understand were not telling everything there was to be told. I saw that every story grew on top of another story, covered it up, and telling one thing was always a way of not telling something else. Sometimes I wanted to pry underneath, to dig up those stories that were buried under the layers. But that was for the most part an idle desire. I did little to seek out the hidden stories. I had enough to keep me busy with the ones that were obvious. Even when I got the sense that things were being deliberately kept from me, I didn't particularly mind. I had my own secrets—who I liked, what I *really* wanted to be when I grew up, my lists of sins and misdemeanours—and I had to assume that others were the same. If they let me keep my secrets, I was more than willing to let them have theirs.

I suppose all of that explains why I grew up in such remarkable ignorance of my hometown's past. I had only the vaguest idea how it had come to be what it was, and I didn't know what had been there before. I believed that Meadow Lake was a place of the new, a place of memories but not history. This was I think the prevailing view in the town. Even the 1885 rebellion seemed to have happened somewhere else, though we were only an hour's drive from Steele Narrows, where the final battle of the uprising had been fought. Mom and Dad had taken us to Steele Narrows several times, and they had pointed out the white crosses on the forested hills there, and they had even told us about Big Bear and Major Steele and Gabriel Dumont. But it didn't seem possible to me; it felt like only another game of cowboys and Indians. Glenn and Michelle and I were more interested in climbing the hundreds of hewn-wood steps to the top of the lookout hill, and picking strawberries or blueberries or chokecherries depending on the season, and searching the tall grass for snakes. We had found a red-eyed garter snake there once, and Mom and Dad had allowed us to bring it home and keep it in a wooden box in the garage. Mysteriously, it had disappeared by the next morning.

I didn't really believe in history, not history *here*. But there were stories about the old days, which meant the era of my grandparents, when it seemed that Saskatchewan had burst into existence fully formed, complete with drought and grasshoppers and ten-cents-a-bushel wheat. And even if that was something of an exaggeration, I was absolutely certain that the Depression had given birth to Meadow Lake, if not to the entire province. To some extent this was true: many of our homesteaders had come north after giving up on other homesteads in the south, when the drought had decimated their crops. During the thirties, Meadow Lake was renowned in Saskatchewan as the place that got rain. Pioneers arrived in droves, claiming new homesteads and starting again the arduous process of turning a foreign place into a home. There were so many of them, and they had such an effect on the landscape and the culture of Meadow Lake, that I suppose I can forgive myself for having once believed that the home-steaders were the first inhabitants of the area.

Certainly, homesteading stories were the closest thing to our creation myths. I couldn't imagine what would have existed in Meadow Lake before the homesteaders came and cleared the land, broke the soil, built roads, dug wells. The reminders of their labour still dotted the landscape: ruins of sod-roofed log cabins, swaybacked windowless barns, rusted threshing machines that looked like mechanical horses. Our old folks' home, the Pioneer Lodge, was filled with the pioneers them-selves. In school we were encouraged to interview a few home-steaders about the old days, and we dutifully blitzed the seniors' residences, collecting reminiscences of tree felling, stump pulling, harvest, community dances. The most shocking thing we discovered was how astonishingly low the prices of eggs and nails and flour and cars had been in the old days.

"D'you know, I remember when a pound of butter was three cents."

"Ho*leeee!*"

All of us dazzled by the miracle of inflation.

We were also taken on field trips to the "Western Development" museums in North Battleford and Lloyd-minster and Saskatoon, all of which contained acres of home-steading paraphernalia, from hand-plows to steam engines to replica prairie towns, complete with grain elevators. This, I thought, is where Saskatchewan came from: this collection of obsolete gadgets, makeshift agricultural implements, musty clothes, and taxidermically preserved animals. The story these museums suggested was one of unending progress, leading from the dark ages of the Depression to our current prosperity, and looking forward to a future as blandly idyllic as the ones in my favourite science fiction comics. I believed it, along with everyone else, because there were no obvious alternatives.

It was only much later that I realized how much had been left out of this story. No one told me, for instance, that Meadow Lake had been a settlement of sorts for at least a hundred years before the arrival of the first homesteaders. Peter Fiddler had established a short-lived Hudson's Bay Company fur-trading post there in 1795. Later in the nineteenth century, it became a Metis settlement, presided over by the patriarch Cyprien Morin and his many descendants. And always of course it was part of the Cree territory too. That was easy to forget.

I didn't know that the people of the Flying Dust Reserve had been relocated there from several small Cree communities in 1878 to make a band in conformity with the regulations of Treaty No. 6. I thought the Crees had always lived there at the mouth of the Meadow River, on "their" land. I didn't really understand that a few generations earlier, all of it was theirs. And I didn't know that the people of Flying Dust, like most other Native people in Canada, were for decades virtually locked within the boundaries of their reserve, subject to the authority of Indian agents who enforced curfews, recorded their activities in logbooks, and sent their children away to residential schools. I didn't know that at the height of Meadow Lake's homesteading boom, the village council sent a petition to Ottawa requesting that the Flying Dust Reserve be relocated to make room for the growing population of settlers. But for the petition to be granted, Chief Gregoire Matchee was required by law to sign it, and he respectfully declined.

For years and years, no one told me any of this.

Muskeg and pond at the Height of Land.

THE HEIGHT *of* LAND

South of Meadow Lake is a bluish line of spruce-covered hills that stretches across the horizon to form a thin boundary between the town and the rest of the world. It divides the north from the south, parkland from prairie, wilderness from civilization. When I was growing up, we thought of it not as a group of individual hills but rather as a single entity, which we called the Height of Land—usually pronounced "heighthaland." A century and more ago, the French and Metis people called it *l'hauteur de terre*. It has always been a crucial boundary, marking the division between the two major watersheds of the province: the Saskatchewan River system to the south and the Churchill River system to the north. These two watersheds are different worlds, with distinct climates, geographies, ecosystems, and cultures. Early explorers are said to have acknowledged the significance of the transition between these territories by stopping to make offerings and prayers when they crossed the Height of Land. They probably learned this practice from their Native guides.

For me, the Height of Land was more of a cognitive construct than a geological formation. As far back as I can remember, it was the most important defining feature of what was home and what was not. It was the place of transition between our way of life and all the incomprehensible ways of life that I imagined, and sometimes saw, in the outside world. But it was always an elusive boundary, one that slipped away as we approached. When we drove up into the hills on our way to Saskatoon, it seemed like just another forest to pass through—a beautiful forest, certainly, and the site of our annual Christmas tree search, which we looked forward to every year—but it was not significantly different from the forests we often saw farther north: poplar, tamarack, spruce, an occasional herd of startled white-tailed deer. But when I looked at the Height of Land from town, it became an imaginary place that appeared to hover above us, like something from *Gulliver's Travels* or *Battlestar Galactica*. Especially on the hottest summer afternoons, it seemed to levitate there, just beyond the wheatfields and pastureland south of town.

I wondered if this feat of levitation was why they called it the Height. The name bothered me, since it suggested that the land where we lived didn't quite measure up. Dad had told me that all the land around Meadow Lake had once been an immense lake, an inland sea. This was why the land was so fertile, he said: because it contained thousands of years' worth of loon shit. He was convinced that the bottom of every lake was blanketed with eons of accumulated loon droppings, which was the reason he usually gave for refusing to swim whenever we were at the cabin. Why he blamed the loons I don't know. He had nothing against them in other respects.

I tried to imagine everything to the north of the Height

of Land covered in water, for dozens, maybe hundreds of miles. It wasn't such a difficult image to conjure, since the west side of town was a swamp already, and the streets were all quagmires in the spring, and everyone complained about water in their basements. One spring a huge flood inundated all the fields in the municipality, from Neeb to Makwa. Except for the protruding grid of the gravel roads, you could have mistaken the whole district for a lake. I remember driving along those roads, listening to one of Dad's *National Geographic* lectures about the rice paddies of China. It was no accident, he said, that wild rice grew so well in northern Saskatchewan.

It was true: land and water are on familiar terms up there. Not far north of town is the beginning of the muskeg, the bogs that stretch for many miles, into the northernmost reaches of the province. Muskeg is a thin layer of turf floating on the water, an earthy membrane that fuses land and liquid. The result is a quivering, rollicking landscape. I imagine Lewis Carroll had muskeg in mind when he wrote in "Jabberwocky" that the "slithy toves / Did gyre and gimble in the wabe." Gyring and gimbling is exactly what muskeg does when you step on it. The reeds move sideways, the cattails bow compulsively and repetitively, the toadstools shiver. We often canoed out to a favourite bog near our cabin and bounced on the muskeg like a trampoline. One time when four or five of us were bouncing simultaneously, Glenn edged over to a weak spot and disappeared. Luckily we were wearing our life jackets. When his head bobbed back through the hole, I grabbed him by the shoulder and we pulled him out—the Creature from the Black Lagoon, covered in muck and weeds, smelling of swamp gas. It was our last experiment in muskeg bouncing.

We came by this pastime honestly. Dad had told us marvellous stories about the muskeg way up north at Cree Lake, where he had gone fly-in fishing before we were born. He said that in storms, pieces of muskeg would dislodge from the edge of the lake and then float around all summer, becoming portable islands.

"They even had trees!" he said. "Tamaracks, and willows, and blueberry bushes. The trunks of these trees would sway in the waves like the mast of a sailboat, and you could see the tamarack roots dangling out behind the island as it floated along. And under these islands, between the snaggly roots, hundreds of huge, *enormous*, IMMENSE jacks were hiding. . . ."

Judging by the extravagance of the stories, it was the best fishing Dad ever had in his life. Of course it was always hard to tell how much of the objective truth was in Dad's stories. He seemed not to recognize the difference between fact and fiction much of the time, and after a while we stopped asking him to make that distinction. We came to see that a story was simply a story, and was all the more valuable for that—far more relevant and vital than a fact, a statistic, a piece of corroborating evidence.

Dad said the guide positioned their boat near one of these islands, and every time the fishermen cast toward it, those leviathan pike would glide out from under the floating turf and attack their lures. It was an absurd, delirious pandemonium of angling, so far from the usual contemplative pastime that it could have been a completely different sport. Maybe alligator wrestling, or shark baiting. Grown men hollered at each other and at the water, calling for the net, each trying to lead his own gargantuan beast across the expanse of tumultuous water where four other hooked fish were rocketing back and forth. I can hear Dad saying "Holy sufferin'!" as he often did in his moments of greatest amazement, and I can see him yanking mercilessly at his line, leaning back into it, his poor fibreglass rod wowing to within a millimetre of its life. And all of them grinning like idiots as they grunted and yelled and tried to steer their monstrous pike away from each other. It was the kind of fishing that every angler dreams about, the kind that is probably only possible in northern Saskatchewan.

But there was a problem. Every time they hooked a truly huge fish, it headed straight for the tamarack roots, rolled around them, and broke the line. This happened time and again. Sometimes they saw a fish attacking one of their Len Thompson red-and-whites with another identical hook still dangling from its mouth. These behemoths were dragging tackle and line around as if it was jewellery, as if they were *collecting* it on purpose.

Dad's line had broken off eight or nine times— twice from casting too far and catching the island itself, the rest of the times from hooking these monster fish and losing them in the roots. He inspected his reel and calculated that he had only about forty feet of line left. Even worse, he had only two more hooks, and the other guys refused to share, having lost dozens of lures themselves.

Then he got an idea. He told the guide to take him right up to the island, and the guide did so, manoeuvring through the roots, lifting the engine halfway up to keep the prop out of the weeds. Dad stepped over the side with one foot to test the muskeg. It swayed here and there but was basically solid. Like an iceberg. A landberg. So he got out, pushed the boat off, and gingerly circumnavigated the island, searching for the two hooks he had lost there. He did find one of them— a lucky red-and-white—dangling from a willow branch, and he tied it to the remainder of his line.

As the other guys kept casting back toward him, hooking the big ones and then losing them in the roots, Dad went straight for the middle of the island and dug his heel into the turf. It gave way, gradually, and after a minute of tentative digging he had opened a hole in the muskeg. He gazed down into the murky water as bits of dislodged turf sunk into invisibility. Then he lowered his hook down into that hole, like an ice fisherman. He liked to claim, in fact, that he had invented a new sport, that he was the world's first and only dirt fisherman.

Certainly he was the most successful one. When he felt the first tug, he hauled on that rod with all his strength and backpedalled recklessly to the edge of the quaking island. The fish—a 29-pound pike—was up on the muskeg before it knew what had happened.

"And did that thing have teeth!" he would say. "Eeeyike. Forty-two rows, right back to his tonsils."

That was Dad's biggest fish, caught through a hole in the earth, dragged up from the most impregnable lair in piscatorial history. He had pictures of the fish to prove his catch— old black-and-whites with him squinting in the sunlight and grinning like a four-year-old as he held that immense shark-like beast across his chest. There were no pictures of the island, but we never thought to question that part of the story. After all, up north anything was possible. In a place where even the land wasn't necessarily land, there was no need for solid grounding in facts.

There is no muskeg south of the Height of Land. Most of the bogs have been drained in the name of agricultural productivity, and even in the southern lakes it's difficult to find enough water to float an island on. There is a corresponding psychological difference between the south and the north too. In the south, facts matter more than stories. It's the realm of statistics, of money, of opportunity. It was where we kids were expected to go when the time came for us to get an education, build a career. I admit it was alluring in its own way. The most visible symbols of its attractiveness were the radio and television relay towers that were perched on the highest hilltops of the Height of Land. They had been there since before I was born, and in the era before satellite communication they were our only real link to the world—a one-way link, since the rest of the world seemed to care little or nothing about what happened on our side of the Height of Land. Most of the time we didn't mind it that way. That line of hills kept us hidden from everyone else, but that hiddenness had a value: it gave us the status of a secret community. We always knew, growing up, that nobody who was anybody would ever come to Meadow Lake, but this also meant that the place was all ours.

Still, there was the call of the south, as represented by those thin towers that reached up to the sky from the Height of Land. At night they were lit with slowly flashing red and white lights that blinked enticingly down on us like advertisements: this way to civilization! Anyone who dreamed of escape would have had these relentless beacons as a symbol of their aspirations—a reminder of the skyscrapers and sparkling lights of the city. Whenever we drove south into the Height of Land, I held a silent observance as those flashing towers approached. When we passed beneath them, we left the north behind.

But the best thing about the Height of Land was coming home through it. I always looked forward to the moment when the town would come into view below us, framed between the jagged shapes of intervening spruce trees, looking like a rather uninspired model-train-set town, the kind that came with the train and required little effort in the way of setup. Virtually none of the prairie towns offer you the luxury of an elevated perspective on them, but the Height of Land gave us one, and it made me see Meadow Lake differently than I otherwise would have—made it look neater and quieter and certainly less active than it really was. I saw that the town was very small, and perhaps even a little ridiculous. But at the same time the perspective from the Height of Land was comforting—it gave me the chance to see that our little enclave was still safe from the rest of the world. I could see the grid of streets, and the church steeples and the flattened oval of the stampede grounds racetrack. Sometimes I thought I could see our house, but I've tried it many times since then and I realize now that it must have been my imagination.

In more recent years, the most visible sign of Meadow Lake from the Height of Land vantage point has been the plume of steam that rises from the pulp mill a few miles east of town. Before that, the major landmarks of the town were the row of broad-shouldered, brightly painted, hundred-foot-tall grain elevators that signalled the existence of a prosperous community. These buildings, like the communications towers, might have been built in the spirit of skyscraper envy—I know of no real reason that they need to be built so tall. We have always reached upward in our architectural aspirations in Saskatchewan, perhaps in answer to the flatness of the land. The other most noticeable structure in town was, of course, another tower: the water tower, a great tin ellipsoid with MEADOW LAKE emblazoned on the south-facing curve. All of the essentials—grain, water, and television—were transported via the sky.

At night, the view of town from the Height of Land was even more spectacular. The distant streetlights would appear below us, arrayed like a constellation. This was my home, reduced to its simplest features, transformed into a pattern rather than a place. It looked warm, and static, and safe.

At the same time, though, I knew it was none of those things. Even back in the early years, when we never locked our doors and when we shuddered at the corruption and crime in the cities, Meadow Lake was far from being a safe place. The murder rate was inordinately high, and we were rumoured to have the highest proportion of police officers to citizens of any town in the province. In the late sixties, the *Saskatoon Star-Phoenix* ran a story about Meadow Lake entitled "Dodge City of the North." I didn't read the article myself until much later, but I heard that it painted Meadow Lake as the last frontier town, a place in which gambling and gunfights and racially motivated violence were common. People in town talked about it for years afterward. Some were insulted to be tarred with the same brush as the "criminal element." The town council worried that the headline would affect the business climate. I think a lot of people just laughed at it, and I imagine that many others, like me, felt a perverse civic pride that our town should be labelled such a wild and unruly place in the eyes of the world. I thought maybe the Height of Land was there to protect the rest of the world from *us*, rather than the other way around. Certainly, to be living in the Dodge City of the north was a compliment to my boyish idea of myself: anyone who survived in such a place must necessarily be tough. I lived in the wild west, or rather the wild north—a place made exhilarating by its connection to Hollywood stereotypes.

Still, I knew the outside world was bristling with perils too, and that the Height of Land offered us little protection. The Cold Lake Air Base was not far away, and one of my less idealistic teachers had pointed out that surely some of the Soviet nuclear arsenal was aimed there. I had seen the films about nuclear winter, and even in primary school I had a taste for apocalyptic science fiction. I imagined that anyone who was looking toward Cold Lake at the time of the explosions would be instantly blinded. It would take a little longer for the rest of the devastation to arrive. Our isolation would, at best, buy us a few extra minutes of existence.

Even the Height of Land itself was dangerous. In 1978, four of Meadow Lake's most prominent businessmen were killed when their plane crashed into one of the highest hilltops. They had been flying back from a football game in

Regina, in a Cessna that one of them owned. No one knows exactly what happened, but there was a story that the pilot, flying in the dark on a cloudy night, had not compensated enough for the height of the hills.

After the accident, the authorities put new lights on one of the Height of Land towers, much brighter ones that went off like tiny, brilliant explosions every three seconds. There have been no aircraft accidents since then, but the lights were so intense that they became notorious for blinding motorists who passed by, and they had to be turned down to a slightly more manageable intensity. Now they're not much brighter than they were when I was a child, and they blink down on the town with the same persistent rhythm they always had. But since the accident, those lights mean something different than they did before. They are no longer beacons of civilization, markers of our place of safety. Instead of beckoning to us, they have become a warning, a monument, a *memento mori* written in code.

Fire at the sawmill, 1995.

THE SCORCHER

If Meadow Lake is the land of muskeg and rain and lakes, it is also the land of fire. This was impossible to forget, surrounded as we were by millions of acres of fuel. Even in its full midsummer lushness—and even in winter—the forest always represented the potential for absolute destruction. We knew it was only a matter of time before the fateful conditions were met and the flames would charge through the north unrestrained, exploding in treetops, leaping roads and rivers and firebreaks, cartwheeling through the underbrush. While the town would probably be saved by the barrier of farmland around it, the rest of the north would be utterly transformed in a matter of days. Our cabins, our favourite picnic spots, our hunting grounds, our scenic roads and walking trails and lakeshores: all of it would be gone.

I never saw a real wildfire in action—at least not at the peak of its intensity, and not close up. But the evidence of fire was everywhere. Almost every spring there was smoke in the air—not wispy, localized plumes like that of a campfire, and not the black, choking smog that hung over the fields every fall when the farmers burned their chaff after harvest. This was a more insidious smoke, a more permeating one. It was so fully suffused into the air that we usually couldn't locate it, couldn't separate it from the rest of the atmosphere.

We could smell it, though: a distinctive spicy odour, with a hint of pine tar, volatile resins vapourized into the air like some colossal and hellish potpourri.

"A big burn somewhere," people would say, tasting the air, gazing contemplatively northward, as if they could pinpoint the source by its signature of smell.

Smoke was the medium we lived in during fire season, sometimes for weeks at a time. We breathed it. It soaked into our clothes. Usually we couldn't see it at all, except perhaps as a slight haze in the distance, a blurring of the Height of Land. It was only at sunrise and sunset that it became luridly, spectacularly visible. As the sun declined to an oblique angle and shone through more and more atmosphere, the smoke caused a red shift in the sky, a vibrant staining of the clouds and of the whole landscape beneath. The sun glowered through the filtration of smoke particles, looking more than ever like a ball of fire, a glowing cinder perched on the horizon. It was like the wildest dream of a black-velvet landscape painter. Although some people called it beautiful, it always made me think of war and battlefields, especially the Technicolor movies of World War II that I had seen on TV. It was the kind of sun that presided over death.

I also saw the aftermath of forest fires several times in my northern travels. Once, on our way to Amyot Lake, we passed through a burn so recent that many tree roots were still flaming, and in places smoke spewed out of the ground. For miles there was nothing but blackened earth, rocks split open in the heat, naked trees standing wide-armed as if in embarrassment. The transparency of the forest was uncanny. You could see deep into the bush, but there was almost nothing to see. No birds or animals or flowers or berries; only the endless variations on black. And the silence. Even the wind made no sound in the leafless branches. The trees became their own tombstones, standing in craggy reminiscence of themselves.

Another persistent reminder that we lived in fire country was the house-sized billboard propped at the edge of a pine forest in the middle of the Height of Land, containing a message outlined in gigantic red letters: "DON'T LET 'THE SCORCHER' STRIKE!" The Scorcher himself dominated the sign: a naked, smirking, red-skinned comic-book devilkin with orange and yellow flames bursting out of his head. The Scorcher's eyes were the most successful representation of mischief I had ever seen, expressing a combination of askance malevolence and caught-in-the-act startlement. In one hand he clutched a lit match, which he held down toward the lower edge of the billboard, as if to ignite the real forest in the background.

This was exactly the kind of cretin who would start a fire, we believed. But Glenn and Michelle and I loved the Scorcher even as we scorned him. His defiant flouting of the most sacred rule of our fire-paranoid culture made him attractive, as only a bad-boy rebel can be. He made arson seem almost fun. We also looked forward to seeing the Scorcher on our long journeys back from Saskatoon because he was the first sign that we would soon be cresting the Height of Land and beginning the descent toward home.

He was the gatekeeper of the north, the usher and gargoyle and menacing giant who signalled to everyone that *this* was a place where things were different. This was the kingdom of fire.

As we approached the sign, we chanted "Scorcher, Scorcher, Scorcher" in the back seat, to Mom and Dad's unconcealable chagrin. We pretended to strike matches and hold them down toward the carpeted hump on the floor of the car. At night the Scorcher would leap into our headlights without warning, dazzling us with his gleaming eyes, his flickering match. We always tried to stay awake so we could have the honour of spotting him first.

"There he is!" someone would shriek.

"I saw first!"

"Did not."

"I—"

"No way, *I* did—stamp stamp no erasies black jack king and queen's honour nineteen seventy si-ix!"

That usually settled the matter.

Sometime in the eighties, the Scorcher was removed from the billboard and replaced by the blander and more authoritarian Smokey the Bear, accompanied by the stern slogan, "IF YOU PUT IT OUT WE WON'T HAVE TO." It was the end of an era. Someone in the Ministry of Natural Resources must have decided that the Scorcher—by then the unofficial guardian and mascot of the north—was just too damned attractive. He was not a positive role model for impressionable youth, who were of course known to have pyromaniacal tendencies already. It was imperative that the Scorcher be replaced by a humourless autocratic bear wearing a ranger's hat who could cure those youngsters of their firebug habits with little more than a steely glance.

And so it was. Social progress triumphed over imaginative flair. I was crushed. I knew that no kids would keep themselves awake on long journeys just to see Smokey, and no one would have sighting races when *his* sign came into view, and no one would ever pretend to be *him*.

But as I got further from childhood, I began to think the billboard replacement wasn't such a bad idea. I suspect now that I may have been influenced by the Scorcher's example once or twice. When I was five, my friend Jerry and I decided to have a campfire one afternoon, so we stole some matches from his mom and lit a pile of crumpled newspapers in an empty closet down in his parents' basement. It seemed safe. There was no way anyone would see us down there. I pulled the closet door partway closed, so the flickering light would look brighter, would reflect off our faces in the cheerful way of campfires.

"Cooell," Jerry said.

"Neato gweeto."

We warmed our hands over the busy little parcels of flame and wished for marshmallows. The wads of paper crumpled inward, winking with embers. I placed a fresh and hastily crumpled sheet on top.

Then came footsteps on the stairs. Three of them, followed by a pause.

"Jerrrayyy!"

I was sent home for my punishment, while Jerry was detained for his. It was the longest block I had ever walked, staring down between my feet, wondering what was in store for me when I got to the back door, telling myself "we didn't *mean* it" again and again like some pathetic prayer of last resort. Dark flecks of ashes (residue of my futile attempt to stamp out the evidence) trailed behind me on the sidewalk.

"We didn't *mean* it, Mom!" I called through the screen door before I even got inside.

"You're gonna need a better story than that," she said.

I was lucky to get away with a serious talking-to.

Not that I really learned my lesson then—there were still a few experiments with the burning barrel ahead of me, and some misadventures with an astonishingly flammable secret combination of household chemicals. But gradually I began to understand how serious fire really was in Meadow Lake. Every summer, the stories of new bush fires raged almost as rapidly and as intensely as the fires themselves. People speculated about the cause of each blaze: lightning, or camp-fires, or cigarettes tossed out the windows of cars, or foolish boys playing with matches. Or Indians. Those who needed someone to blame usually focused on the Natives. "Black lightning," they would say, shaking their heads in disgust. It took me years to figure out what that meant. The belief was that Indians in the north set forest fires on purpose so they could create high-paying jobs for themselves as firefighters. There was never any evidence to support this, but still the prejudice persisted.

For Dad the real culprits were careless campers. He was obsessed with the idea that someone's stray campfire would inevitably burn down the entire northern forest. Whenever he caught the first whiff of a fire in the air, he would say, "Careless camper, I bet," with a particular tone of

world-weary resignation. He swore we would never be guilty
of such accidental arson. After our picnic wiener roasts, our
fresh pickerel shore lunches, our evening bonfires at the
cabin, he would throw shovels full of sand on the embers and
then pour buckets of water on the mixture and stir it with a
stick. Ash stew. I was always amazed at how the seemingly
dead coals would burst and simmer when water touched
them. When I was allowed to pour, I dropped the water in a
slow drizzle, pretending to be a World War II pilot on a
strafing run. Puffs of smoke erupted out of the ground, even
in places that had already been liberally watered.

It turned out that Dad had good reasons for his legendary precautions. He told us that embers could keep burning underground, following a tree root like a slow-motion
fuse, and the fire could leap to the surface days or even weeks
later. Mom even corroborated this, telling us about the
ground fires she had seen as a girl, when the homesteaders
burned their brush piles in bonfires. Long after the brush
piles were gone, the ground beneath them continued to
smoulder. Rain and even snow couldn't stop it. Sometimes
the smoke disappeared altogether for days before it returned.
And at any time the fire could flare up—sometimes a good
distance from the source, because it crept along underground,
burning buried moss and twigs and grass, and even the soil
itself, until it found its way back to the surface. Flame blooming out of the ground like mushrooms. People would come
with blankets or buckets of water and try to put it out, but
they had to be careful because new fires could pop up right at
their feet. I imagined their ginger fire dances, hopping
around like Jack-Be-Nimble as they swung their pails to and

fro. Often, Mom said, they just had to stand back and let those underground fires burn themselves out.

I thought about the earth itself on fire, becoming embers that breathed and glowed in the wind, smouldering through spring rains or November snowfalls, burning so subtly that no one noticed. I stared at the ground sometimes—in our garden, or out in the vacant lot across from the town hall—and I wondered what was underneath. I sniffed for smoke. Any place could be burning without us even knowing it.

Fire was a constant threat to our existence, but at the same time it had also made my home possible. I didn't understand this until I learned about the Great Fire of 1919, which burned much of northern Saskatchewan and Alberta in two continuous months of flames. It was the largest forest fire in the history of either province, and the one that led to the creation of full-time firefighting brigades in the north. For weeks its smoke was as thick as a fog in Regina, and it was said to be visible as far south as Oklahoma. And yet even this extraordinary cataclysm was an untold story in Meadow Lake, one that I stumbled upon in adulthood when researching the town's history. Someone showed me a transcript of a homesteader's account of "the Big Fire," and I was astounded. This fire had shaped the entire northern forest that I grew up in, but somehow at the age of twenty-eight I had never even heard of it.

By that time, most of the witnesses to the fire were gone, but I found a few of them as I travelled through the north. Kate Cossette of Canwood, who was ninety-nine years old when I met her, told me about the evacuation of the town of

Big River: the flames roaring in the distance, all the women and children crowded onto the last train, leaving their belongings behind—and leaving also their men, who had been commandeered to fight the fire with pitchforks, shovels, axes, and only bandannas tied over their faces for protection. She had just gotten married, and when she said goodbye to her husband at the train it was as if he was going off to war. She didn't see him for three weeks. The fire was their honeymoon.

Elizabeth Bouvier was a child in the residential school at Beauval—about a hundred miles north of Big River—when the fire came through. She remembered the sky getting so dark with smoke that the nuns who ran the school had to light candles in the middle of the day.

"I didn't think all that much of it at the time," she said, "didn't know how dangerous it was. But since then I have this fear, a fear of wind. Because when the fire was burning there in the distance, it created this huge wind, like a storm, with lightning flashing through the smoke. Even now when there's lightning I close the blinds in my apartment. Seventy-five years ago it happened, and still I close my blinds."

The fire burned several communities, most notably the town of Lac la Biche, Alberta. It didn't reach Meadow Lake, but it virtually surrounded the town at various points in the summer. Men went to fight fire at Island Hill to the east and Chitek Lake to the south. A wall of flame was visible in the west for several days. Mary Gehl, who still lives on her parents' homestead just out of town, told me she had memories of a false sunset that kept burning on the western horizon through the night. George Stewart, who lived ten miles west of town, is said to have spent one whole day on top of his sod-roofed barn, standing with buckets of water that he dumped on the flying cinders as they landed in the dry grass there. They were like swarms of burning insects. After the wind changed direction and that particular part of the fire burned itself out, Stewart learned that it had never got closer than seven miles from his place. Those cinders had flown a whole league, borne eastward by the fire's own blasting storm wind, before they touched down on the roof of his barn. It was no wonder this became known as the fire that came from the sky.

There were many stories of narrower escapes than this: of people huddling down in swamps as flames roared through the crowns of the trees above them; of a group of Jehovah's Witnesses who thought the apocalypse had come; of a family who returned to their burned farmhouse to find that their stash of silver coins in the cellar had melted together into a lump; of farmers and ranchers releasing their frenzied animals into the forest and never seeing them again; of deer, moose, and bear charging into towns, seeking shelter from the oncoming smoke and flames. And several people died in the fire—we will never know exactly how many. Most of them were Native, according to the accounts. One report, recorded in Joseph Dion's *My Tribe the Crees,* tells the story of a Cree family caught in the fire near the shore of Lac des Isles. They tried to take shelter in the muskeg, digging themselves down into the watery turf, covering their backs with what blankets they had. But it wasn't enough. Two of them were dead by the time the flames passed over them, and three more died in the following days, their lungs scorched, their skin falling off.

The Great Fire was a disaster for everyone in the north, but it was far more cataclysmic for the Native people, who depended on the forest for most of their livelihood. With much of the habitat for game destroyed, their food supply dwindled drastically. The fur trade, too, was effectively ended for many years, and the Crees and Metis were cast more and more upon the charity of the government.

And in the following years, when the homesteaders began to arrive in Meadow Lake in increasing numbers, the fire had made it much easier for them to clear the land, build roads, and create settlements. In the ashes of the fire the place became a different place, with new inhabitants and new stories and new ways of relating to the land. And these new people were so driven, and so deeply committed to their mythologies of progress and their sense of destiny, that most of them and their descendants eventually forgot what had been there before. They even forgot the story of the fire.

Cariou family reunion at the farm.

THE BLOOD MAGNET

In my first few years I never thought to ask *why* I was from Meadow Lake. It seemed inevitable that I should be who I was, where I was. But as I heard more stories about the time before my birth, I began to entertain the ominous possibility that things might have been different. Like all stories, the events could have veered off in any direction at any moment, leaving me changed. I marvelled at the coincidences, the improbabilities, that had made me into myself. For example: if my mom hadn't become a nurse, and if my dad's mother hadn't remarried, I would never have lived in Meadow Lake, and I might not have existed at all.

Mom and Dad grew up hundreds of miles apart, and they met only when circumstances brought them to an obscure little town in the northwestern reaches of the province. Mom had just finished training to be a registered nurse, first in Prince Albert and then in Saskatoon. She had moved to Meadow Lake for her first job, a one-year position as a public health nurse, after which she planned to return to Saskatoon for further training. Dad had moved to Meadow Lake a few years earlier to article with the town's only lawyer,

Herb Cathrea. He worked in an office above the pool hall just off Main Street, looking out on the Empire Hotel, which later became notorious but was probably almost respectable in 1964. Dad's main reason for coming to Meadow Lake was that his mother, Marie Clemence, had remarried a few years earlier and had moved up there to live with her new husband, Alec Laliberte, and his family. She and her husband (her kids called him Pop) both worked the concession at the golf course, and they took in children who were orphaned or estranged from their families. Dad's brothers Leo, Vic, and Charlie had gone to Meadow Lake along with their mother, so for Dad the town might have been the closest thing to a family home, now that the farm at Ituna had been sold. He probably felt lucky to land an articling position there.

Many others might have thought differently, given the town's isolation, the interminable winters, the dilapidated roads, and the plagues of insects that rose up out of the bogs each spring like biblical anathemas. But he had grown up with hardship, as one of fifteen children raised by a widow in the wake of the Depression, and his own hometown had also been humble. Before he arrived in Meadow Lake he had visited it numerous times, and he would have known almost immediately that it had the elements he would find essential in a home: beautiful country to roam in, plenty of good hunting and fishing, a bustling community. I think when he moved there he was hoping to stay.

Mom and Dad met by accident, as they liked to tell us in later years. I tried to imagine it as a spectacular collision, symbolizing the dangerous randomness of love. But it was only a fender-bender. In fact, that was all I really knew about it for certain. By the time I was thirteen I had heard various mutually contradictory accounts of the story, so I fabricated my own version, which turned out to be only slightly less fanciful than the adventures of Simpleton Simon Sasquatch. In my family, the absence of certainty has never got in the way of a story.

This particular account of my prehistory began with Mom preparing for a blind date, arranged by her friend Inga. She had borrowed Inga's car to drive downtown to buy some nail polish, and as she was pulling out of her parking spot near Madill's Drugs, her front bumper scraped a long divot in the door of a red Mercury Comet.

"*Uffda feeda*," I imagined her saying. In times of crisis, she often reverted to her mother's universal Norwegian expression of dismay.

What to do? No one was in the other car, and she couldn't wait around for the owner to return because she had to get ready for her date. So she scribbled a note of apology on the back of her drugstore sales receipt, along with her name, driver's licence and phone number. She hurried back to her apartment, phoned Inga about the accident, which luckily hadn't damaged Inga's car, and then continued her regimen of beautification.

Her date arrived just after seven. Mom wanted to leave the apartment immediately because she knew the phone might ring at any moment and she would have to appease the irate car owner. It was awkward enough to meet a new man without having to worry about a telephone confrontation. So she ushered this new guy down the stairs before they had even properly said hello.

She began to relax a little when they got outside and began walking. It was a warm June evening, and the mosquitoes weren't as bad as they could have been, and the sun was still so high that it was hard to imagine night would ever come. They were supposed to meet Inga and her boyfriend at the Lariat Lunch for supper, but first they walked twice around the block, talking about their families and their hometowns. Then he led her to his car and opened the passenger door for her.

She stopped.

"What's wrong?" he asked.

It was a red car—memorably red. Mom walked slowly, cringing, around the front of the vehicle to inspect the driver's door. There was the gouge.

When she looked back at Dad, he was holding up her scribbled note, grinning the first of his trademark grins he ever gave her.

"Lucky thing you know a good lawyer," he said.

They were married the following year, not in Meadow Lake but in Prince Albert, closer to Mom's family. Her father refused to attend the ceremony because he was resolutely opposed to having a Catholic in the family—especially a Catholic like my dad, who had nearly decided to become a priest. But they went ahead with the wedding despite Grandpa's disapproval, and the families welcomed them with a raucous celebration that eventually spilled out into the Canwood Hotel, where several of my aunts- and uncles-to-be partied long into the night, one of Dad's sisters went into labour, and a few of the wedding guests committed tomfooleries that are only hinted at even today.

Slightly more than a year later, I came dutifully into the world, unaware of the contingencies and inevitabilities that had contributed to my existence. The apartment was full of relatives for months, according to Mom. But the situation changed quickly. Just before I was born, Grandma Laliberte and Pop had gone to Vancouver to care for her oldest daughter, Sandy, who was dying of multiple sclerosis, and they never moved back. In the early spring of 1968, Pop died suddenly when he and Grandma were driving to Meadow Lake for a visit. After his funeral, she decided to return to Vancouver.

Without their matriarch, the remaining Cariou relatives soon dispersed from Meadow Lake, going to Saskatoon or Edmonton in search of opportunity. We might have moved too. But Mom and Dad had the promise of careers in Meadow Lake, and they had made some good friends there, and the town wasn't too far from Mom's relatives in Canwood. They had already bought a house, and perhaps even then they harboured thoughts that they might be able to live on a farm someday if they stayed in this area where land was so plentiful. And I think they also felt a more personal affinity for the place itself: its tumultuous seasons, its wilderness, its unmappable skies. They wanted to stay.

So it happened that I came to call this place home. Mom and Dad chose it for me.

But that knowledge didn't fully answer my questions about where I came from and why. I wondered what it was that held me to my parents—or to any of my family—and the myriad choices they had made in the past. I wanted to have some say in the matter, to plant my own flag on my chosen place and claim it as my point of origin. But it didn't work that way. I couldn't choose my family either.

It was something of a consolation to learn that I was not only from Meadow Lake. Through my parents and grandparents, I was from all kinds of other places too—places I had never even seen. When kids at school asked "Where are you from?" they meant "Where is your *family* from?" It was a question of ethnicity, of blood allegiance. Everyone was assumed to have come from somewhere else.

"I'm French, German, and Norwegian," I confidently declared, basing my identification on the accents of my grandparents. Sometimes I added "English" to the list for good measure, even though I saw no evidence of English relatives. Since I spoke the language it seemed natural that there would be a Brit somewhere in the family tree.

I knew almost nothing about those European countries that I claimed as ancestral homelands, but nevertheless I understood that it was important to claim them, to have an uncomplicated answer to that question of allegiance that was thrown out at me so often.

"Where you from again?"

"Norwayfrancenglandgermany." I spoke it like a password at the gate of a citadel. Sometimes I wondered if there was something more to the question, something I wasn't getting. But my four magic place names always did the trick, so there was no reason to inquire further.

I don't remember any of my grandparents ever speaking about their "old countries," but it was obvious that they were not from here. They still seemed like foreigners to me, even though they were all Canadians by now, and they had lived in the country since before Mom and Dad were born. With Grandma Strelau the foreignness was manifested in the foods she cooked; with Grandpa Strelau it was the German Bible he read; with Grandma Laliberte it was her fervent devotion to Catholicism. All of them had their distinctive accents, their own strange languages, their siblings with whom they spoke in tongues. At family functions I listened to them, bewildered. *I came from this?*

Grandpa Cariou, my dad's dad, had died many years earlier, but I knew that he too had been a foreigner. He was born in Brittany, Dad told me, and then he worked in the cork forests of Algeria before coming to Saskatchewan and marrying Grandma. Dad related his father's descriptions of the cork forest: the looming, craggy-limbed oak trees with thick, thick bark that insulated them so well they could survive the hottest forest fires. The workers stripped these layers of cork off the living trees with hatchets, leaving them pale and glistening—and they survived even this, and grew back another dark coat of cork within a decade. I tried to imagine these trees: the smell of their sap, the sound of their leaves in the wind. The sensation of being peeled; of growing a new skin.

No matter what else my grandparents were, they did have one thing in common: they had all been homesteaders. I could understand that, and could even identify with it to a certain extent, but still it didn't fully alleviate the fact of their strangeness. How could I belong to them if they were so different? Grandpa Strelau sat me on his knee and taught me my *ein zwei dreis,* as I called them, but I had little sense that I was learning something that belonged to me, something of my own heritage. It felt like a party trick, a ruse, as if Grandpa was the ventriloquist and I was the polyglot dummy. I might just as well have been speaking Urdu or Sardinian.

It was even difficult to understand my connection to the many members of my family who obviously weren't foreigners, who spoke like me and who watched the same TV programs as I did. I couldn't see much of a family resemblance between myself and the others, though some people said I looked like Mom. Glenn had red hair like Dad and Uncle Charlie and Aunt Ginger and several of our cousins on the Cariou side. "Sure can tell *you're* a Cariou," people said to him, but never to me. I had no such marker of family belonging. And actually, when I thought of it, neither did most of the relatives. Even Glenn and Michelle and I looked completely different from each other. At weddings and funerals and anniversaries, I surveyed the assembled relatives and wondered what they really had in common, these farmers, oilfield workers, mechanics, carpenters, bank clerks, wheeler-dealers, card sharks, housewives, raconteurs, and retirees. Their hair, their eyes, and even their skin colour were just about everywhere on the spectrum. And yet there was definitely *something* that linked them all together, and linked me to them: some magnetism of the blood or some collective delusion of tribal affiliation. But I couldn't pinpoint it.

My cousins and I were fascinated with family secrets. Not that we knew any, but we knew they must exist, somewhere beneath the garrulous fabric of our family's clanhood. What family *wouldn't* have them? Maybe we kids were sensitized to this because, as recent arrivals in the fold, we knew more clearly than the adults that family was a tenuous arrangement, even an absurd one. Or maybe we were just perverse. We listened for the times when our parents seemed to be talking evasively, referring to things we didn't know. And then we filled in the gaps with speculations. Lies, really. When we ran out of innuendoes, we simply made things up.

"Jolene got pregnant last year from some guy at the Ex, that's why she got to go away for the summer."

"Aunt Louella's a pisstank."

"You ask me, there's something screwy in the family woodpile."

"When cousin Max moved to the city, he as they say took a trip down the old fairy road."

I didn't actually believe these stories, but I was certain there were secrets somewhere in the family. I just knew. My imagination raced over the possibilities. Sometimes on long car trips, my speculations got the best of me and I started wondering whether those two people in the front seat were *really* our parents, or if we had been abducted by some particularly clever imposters. I would ask Mom and Dad questions, to test them, to see if they were themselves. *What day is my birthday? Glenn's? Michelle's? Who's Uncle Eddy married to?* Finally Dad would say, "Enough, now," and I would know it must be him. Nobody else could say that with quite the same bluster as he did.

I also wondered sometimes if *I* was the family secret, if I had been adopted into the family but no one had ever told me. It was possible. I had heard of it happening: people discovering at the age of twenty-five or sixty or ninety that they weren't who they had assumed themselves to be. There were no simple tests of this, no questions that would settle the matter. As I thought about it, I realized I could never be completely sure. I would always have to take someone's word for it that my parents were in fact my parents.

Most of the time, I believed. But what if they were lying? Where would I belong then?

II

ॐ

Where I Touch the Earth

*Leon Sergent's store, 1920. The streets remained
this muddy for sixty-five years.*

HOME FREE

In childhood my truest home was the backyard: sandbox, snowbanks, ice rink, garden, swing set. It was the only place that was unquestionably our own. Glenn and Michelle and I could do pretty much anything we wanted in the yard, as long as the lawn and the flowerbeds remained intact. Like snakes and ladders, we slithered up the towering Russian poplar trees and slipped back down the skin-smooth bark. We lobbed Frisbees and lawn darts and Nerf footballs, we dug down to China in the sandbox, we chanted impromptu rhymes over the repetitive rusty squawk of the chains on our swing set. Every November Dad flooded our garden so we could skate there for the rest of the winter, swatting wild slapshots at chewed-up sponge hockey pucks that buried themselves in the surrounding snowbanks. I used my hockey stick as a crutch, and hoped no one would notice I couldn't skate without it. When the neighbour kids came over we played hockey well into the darkness, until we lost the last of the pucks or until our feet were completely numb. The aftermath was torture: standing on the hot-air register in the kitchen, dancing in agony, wishing to be anywhere else at any other time;

wishing to stay frozen. But the unbearable throbbing, the breakable, crystalline feeling of my toes, could not be willed away. For hours afterward my feet glowed with residual heat.

I remember wandering in the garden in July, eating pods full of peas straight off the vine—opening them with a slight popping sound, prying the pods apart like delicate seashells, scooping all the peas into my mouth by scraping the open pod against my lower teeth. I liked to keep them in my mouth for a long time, rubbing their tiny stems off with my tongue, feeling their coolness dissipate until they no longer seemed to have a temperature. The taste was distant at first; only a hint of sweet grassiness. I savoured the near-intangibility of it. Sometimes I would crunch them all at once and cringe at the overload of flavour. Other times I would store most of them in my cheek and hold one single pea on my tongue, sensing its oblong shape, the scar on it where the stem had been attached. Then, carefully, I would husk it with a gentle bite to the skin, slipping out the tender halves of the inner pea, crunching the skin with my molars and swallowing it while the sweetness flooded my tongue. Those hemispheres of peas were the smoothest things I had ever touched. It seemed a travesty to bite them, so after I had pressed out their flavour on the roof of my mouth, I swallowed them whole, like pills.

Sometimes Glenn came out in the garden with me and both of us ate peas, eyeing each other to be sure we got the same number of pods. Then we got the idea of feeding them to our dog, Pierre, who loved them at least as much as we did, though he never caught on to the idea of savouring them. He would crunch on a pod with it hanging sideways out of his mouth like a cigar—in the manner of Groucho Marx—yet there was always a look of grim intensity on his poodle face. If we reached toward him while he was doing this, he growled so ferociously his whole body quivered. We used to play him like a musical instrument, reaching toward him and away to produce varying degrees of sound. The concert nearly always ended with a bite, and one of us howling an encore all the way to the house.

Unfortunately Pierre liked the peas so much that he started eating them straight off the vine. When we went out to the rows, there were only desiccated green ribbons dangling from the plants. I was blamed for it at first, because I sometimes liked to eat the pods, but eventually I was exonerated when Pierre was stricken with a telltale intestinal disorder.

We loved carrots too, though we preferred the ones grown on the other side of the fence by our neighbours the Carters. We used to climb up on our garbage shed in the corner of the lot and then slide like firemen down the metal pole of their clothesline into the carrot patch. They had several long rows of carrots, all of which looked bigger and more succulent than the stunted ones in our garden. Whenever I slid down, I plucked out four or five carrots and clambered back over the fence for a feast. They definitely tasted better than the ones in our garden: more exotic, more dangerous. And there were so many of them. Hundreds. Millions. I didn't think Mrs. Carter would notice, as long as we left her prize carrot alone. We could see it from the top of the fence, and I had heard her bragging about it to one of the neighbour ladies, Mrs. Beale. It *was* immense. The green top was thick and much taller than all the surrounding vegetables, and the orange root bulged audaciously out of the ground, displaying its enormous girth, like a fat man proud of his belly. It was thicker than even the largest cucumber in the grocery store. We watched its growth all August, as we jumped down into the garden from time to time for a snack, but we never dared to go so far down the garden path as to get a close look at the prize. It was positioned at the end of a row, right in front of Mrs. Carter's kitchen window, and you never knew when she was going to appear there.

Then one day after a rain, my friend Leonard came over, and we stole the carrot. We had dared each other, standing on top of the garbage shed, peering past the reflections on that kitchen window, wondering where Mrs. Carter was.

"Chiggiiin! Bawk bawk."

"No, you."

"No you."

"No YOU."

"Bawk bawk baaaawwwwk."

"YOU."

"YOU."

It escalated for several minutes, and then suddenly Leonard was sliding down the pole and I was right after him, my runners catching on his hands. During the long sprint down the rows he slipped in the mud, so we reached the carrot at the same instant. We both grabbed on to the greens, as low down as we could reach, and we heaved. The carrot came out, miraculously, like Excalibur from the stone.

"Holeeee," Leonard whispered.

We stood there for a second, looking at each other through the swaying carrot foliage, pondering the magnitude of our accomplishment. It was even bigger than I had imagined: a great orange war club, an earthbound zucchini. We tried to run, but so much mud had built up on our shoes that we had to swing our feet like the snowshoe racers at the winter festival. When we reached the fence, Leonard lobbed the carrot over and we scrambled after it.

We were caught, of course. The mudprints on the fence led straight to us: slumped on the other side, hyperventilating, nearly breaking our teeth on the immense woody vegetable. It tasted like a piece of old lumber, a mossy fence post from some abandoned corral. I was almost glad to be caught so I didn't have to take another bite.

Mrs. Carter was the one who caught us, but instead of whaling on us herself, she called Mom outside to look at the spectacle. We hadn't moved since Mrs. Carter's imposing face had appeared at the fence above us. Both of us were paralyzed with fear, and we waited with predestinarian dread for the punishment. Mom saw us there, our feet clogged with mud, our shirts smeared with dirt and bits of carrot. She looked sick. Mrs. Carter pretended to laugh it all off, but it sounded like something between a cough and a shriek, as if she was receiving the Heimlich manoeuvre.

Mom sent Leonard home, and I was required to give back the remains of the gnawed and defoliated carrot. As Mrs. Carter marched out into the alley, she held it far away from herself, as if she was afraid of our germs.

My only punishment was the one I most dreaded. I had to go to confession the next week and broadcast my shame to God:

Bless me Father for I have sinned.
It has been three months since my last confession.

I have coveted my neighbour's carrots and I have stolen them. Amen.

I was amazed to learn that three Hail Marys and three Our Fathers were the price of such a transgression.

Trespassing was a serious issue for me after that. I came to understand that I didn't necessarily belong in whatever places I happened to find pleasant or tempting. There were rules; there were boundaries—and none of them were determined by me. I puzzled about them. If there were places where I didn't belong, there must also be at least one place where others didn't belong, and that place must be mine. But how could I know what it was? Our yard was a safe bet, but what about the rest of our block (not counting the Carter place)? What about my friend Jerry's yard, a block north of us, or Neal's place, a block and a half away?

I thought hard about the criteria for belonging. There was the Lord's Prayer: "Forgive us our trespasses as we forgive those who trespass against us." But it seemed to me that the people I knew were not very forgiving of trespassers. The more convincing rationale, I thought, could be found in the bastardization of a popular song that the neighbourhood boys had taught me:

This land is my land
This land ain't your land
I got a shotgun
And you ain't got one
If you don't get off
I'll blow your head off

This land is PRIvate property
This land is PRIvate property.

That song was our anthem of territorialism, shouted across back lanes and property lines, called out as a taunt by whoever stood at the top of the hill. We claimed places arbitrarily, simply by occupying them. Sometimes the song was a chorus of solidarity, uniting us neighbourhood kids against the outsiders from other parts of town, and sometimes it was an instrument of division, shouted in competition over a particular spot. Whoever voiced the most convincing threat became the arbiter of belonging.

I knew it wasn't like this for everyone. Some people could go anywhere they wanted. Criminals, first of all. People who had guns, or knives, or intimidating fists—people who lived by the code of the song, instead of just singing it. We knew the names of the older boys who had been arrested for breaking and entering, and we knew some who had never been caught. We idolized them a little, for their ability to walk into someone else's house and make it temporarily their own. They were desperadoes, nomads, like so many of the men in the westerns we watched on TV. We didn't want to meet them (and our parents had told us we couldn't), but still we wanted to be like them.

There were other nomads in town who were not considered dangerous—people like Arla Jaynes, who roamed the streets almost every day, talking loquaciously and animatedly to herself. Her wanderings were usually tolerated because she was "differnt," but she paid a heavy price for her freedom. Kids mocked her and mimicked her, and some adults did too. Once I saw her trudging down our back alley with her face held out in front of herself, as if someone was pulling her along with a string. When she got closer I saw why. Blood was coming out her nostrils and dripping from her upper lip. She made no attempt to wipe it off, but she leaned forward so it wouldn't splash on her clothes.

"Those boys I tell you," she was saying—not to me. "Those boys better. Better smarten up or I tell you. Honestly. I mean what'm I, what'm I sposed to do?"

She paused and dabbed at her lip with the back of her hand before answering: "Well, *I*'d tell their mothers. That's what *I*'d do." And then she walked on.

There was another man something like Arla whose nickname was Ranger. I never knew his real name. He lived just out of town in a shack with his aged mother, and most days he walked into town, stopping to look for bottles in the ditches. He went into the Co-op grocery store twice a week, where it was rumoured he only ever bought two items: paper towels and chocolate milk. The kids said, "He stirs 'em together and voila, Ranger Soup."

Ranger's hair was matted, and he smelled—or at least that was what everyone said. Few people got close enough to find out. When he came into the grocery store everyone scattered, and even on the streets people would cross to the other side when they saw him marching along at his distinctive plodding pace, fronds of brown hair flailing, arms perfectly still at his sides. I suppose his reputation for odour saved him from some of the violence that Arla endured, but still he was thoroughly abused. Teenagers yelled at him out their car windows. "Ranger, you stinkin' hog. Take a fuckin' bath, you're peelin' the paint off my car." Kids imitated his loping gait. Mom told us she felt more sorry for him than for anyone in town.

Our favourite wanderer in Meadow Lake was an entirely different kind of nomad, one who was welcome everywhere. Mr. Fontaine, the Rototiller Man, went from house to house every spring and fall offering to till people's gardens for a few dollars. He used one of those stand-up rototillers that looks like a motorized hand-plow, but his tiller was like nothing anyone had ever seen. He had rigged up a platform and three small wheels that he attached to the machine so he could ride it up and down the streets without the tines digging in.

This strange invention became a key to the town. Mr. Fontaine was welcome in the backyards and laneways and side streets of every neighbourhood, and everyone recognized him instantly as he cruised along behind the churning Briggs & Stratton engine. It looked like he was trying to tame some great unruly beast: a snorting, blaring contraption with its menacing row of rotating blades in front. It had only one speed, which was surprisingly fast. We could never keep up to him on our bikes, though we always tried. We followed him by the distinctive clamour of the engine, pedalling as hard as we could, hoping for a glimpse of the Rototiller Man flying along behind those galloping tines like a Roman charioteer, his forearms vibrating crazily. We wanted more than anything to be like him: to be paid for mucking in the gardens of the whole town, to be famous for inventing a new mode of locomotion, to be celebrated as the harbinger of spring and the last visitant of autumn. I firmly believe he was more popular than the mayor, more legendary than any of our sports heroes.

Mr. Fontaine rode that careening tiller for years, until the roads in town were finally paved and some overprotective officials told him he had to stop, in case his tines should damage the asphalt. By then he was ready to retire anyway. He traded the tiller in for a motor scooter, which he still rides to church at the age of ninety-two.

We did our best to follow Mr. Fontaine's example and wander when we could, especially on the days when the mud tempted us. In the early years, Meadow Lake was famous for mud. The roads were pure gumbo, and often cars would come sluicing down our street, their tires so deep in the ruts we wondered how they could move at all. On particularly wet days, they would leave wakes in the muck as they plowed through the biggest potholes in front of our house. The water flew up in dingy waves beside them, like a water skier spraying.

Our ditches were usually at least half full, and the driveway was a quagmire. Mom and Dad were embarrassed when people visited from out of town. But we loved it. We stomped in puddles, waded across ditches, created little rivers between puddles, and sometimes made dams on the trenches that our parents had dug for drainage. We spent most of our time in rubber boots, which were largely ineffective because either they were full of holes or we waded too deep in the puddles. Sometimes for whole summers we would have to put plastic bags on our feet before pulling on our boots. McGavin's Bread bags were particularly popular for this. But they were prone to leaking, and worst of all, they made your feet slide around inside your boots, which were therefore more likely to slip right off at the worst possible moment. The lost boot was a familiar sight: a kid standing one-legged, his bread-bagged foot held out tentatively, balancing himself there and staring back at the empty boot embedded in the muck. It was so common and so comical that we came up with a name for the predicament.

"Andrew flamingoed yesterday in Carlson's ditch, you shoulda seen him standing there crying for his boot. Lost his sock and his bread bag too, and nobody'd get them for him so he had to step in, bare foot and all."

Even as winter approached, the mud stayed with us. There was always a time, usually in late October, when the mud was starting to freeze, and it would bend when we stepped on it. We trudged around deforming the edges of half-frozen tire tracks in the driveway, crushing the newly formed ice in the puddles, and trying our damnedest to stomp down one last footprint into the cooling earth, to make a mark that would last the rest of the winter. Soon the snow would come and obliterate all our efforts until spring, when occasionally in the melt we would see the misshapen remains of what *might* have been, months earlier, one of our footprints.

In winter, we used to play on the boulevard of Main Street, digging tunnels in the banks of snow that the snowplow had left. We used to build up stockpiles of snowballs in our tunnel forts, to throw at each other or occasionally at a passing car, or—if we were particularly daring—at the newly erected town mascot, a larger-than-life fibreglass statue of a bronze cowboy riding an impossibly bucking bronze horse. We would aim for the cowboy's head or his outstretched free hand, which looked like he had just tossed something straight up in the air—perhaps a snowball of his own.

The tunnels were our secret retreats from the world, little nests of comfort that insulated us from cold and wind. I loved the quality of light in them, especially at night, when the walls glowed faintly with the light of the streetlamps above us, as if the snow itself was phosphorescent. We could hardly hear anything from in there, not even the cars driving past a few feet away, and not the voices of the other kids who sometimes organized raiding parties to attack us. The one exception to this silence was the crunching and squealing of snowboots on the snow overhead, which was a warning that we would soon be pelted with snowballs, or that our roof was about to be smashed in.

In summer, when we were tired of the mud, we liked to play with bees. I remember catching bumblebees in a pickle jar with nail holes poked in the lid. Glenn and I pushed dandelion flowers into the jar so our bees would have enough food to provide us with the honey we wanted. I watched them for hours through the distorted, mottled surface of the jar, my eyelashes nearly touching the glass. I was fascinated with their pollen-laden rear legs, dusted with yellow from the insides of flowers.

I was always disappointed that the bees weren't interested in our dandelions. They only crawled along the edges of the glass, their legs moving tentatively, their mandibles opening and closing, their rear-end stingers bobbing slowly up and down against the glass. Occasionally the jar rang with their reverberant buzzing. They were looking for escape. When we saw that no honeycombs were forthcoming, we wanted to release them too—but how? Once you've angered something, how do you free it?

Eventually, I opened the lid partway, and we stood back while Glenn popped it off with a stick. We ran all the way around the block, past clumps of alfalfa with more bees at work in the flowers. When we got back to the jar, we saw that only one bee was gone. The rest of them stayed there for a long time, and eventually we had to turn the jar upside-down to get them out. They fell to the dirt, along with the clump of wilted dandelions, and then they crawled away, as innocuous as caterpillars. No one got stung.

For me, the stings came later, when I fell headfirst onto a hornet's nest. After all our dangerous wanderings, the catastrophe happened at home. It was right below our front steps, and I was showing off, dangling upside down by my knees from the wrought-iron railing. We knew the hornet's nest was down there, even though it was inconspicuous: just a couple of holes in the dirt at the base of the cotoneaster shrubs. We had watched the ferocious-looking, armour-plated hornets fly down into the ground and emerge from it like futuristic warplanes. Maybe my audience of neighbour kids—Kristine, Roger, Bruce, Mildred, Stephen—remembered the hornets, but I must have forgotten. When my legs slipped off the railing I had no idea what was about to happen.

I was stung all over my face, my neck, my scalp. It happened instantly, as if I had completed some kind of circuit and the earth was transmitting a tremendous electric shock to me. That's the only sensation I can compare it to: grabbing an electric fence, sticking a key in the outlet, holding a spark plug while someone cranks the engine. I remember rising up from among the cotoneaster shrubs with a flurry of hornets around me. All the other kids were running down the steps and out onto the lawn, flailing their arms and looking back at me over their shoulders, as if they were more afraid of me than of the hornets.

In a few seconds I could hardly see. My eyes were swelling shut.

I was lucky it was a Saturday and a doctor lived across the street. Mrs. Toews, our babysitter, led me over to Dr. Letkeman's house, and he gave me an injection. I slept for a long time, and when I woke up I could see again. The electric feeling was gone, but it was replaced by more familiar varieties of pain: burning, throbbing, tenderness. Then the door opened and Mom and Dad crept to the foot of my bed. I almost expected them to say "Such a shame" and shake their heads in disbelief, but instead they were nearly smiling around their studied looks of concern.

"Whaff fo fungy?" I said, and at the first syllable I realized how oddly disproportionate I had become. Glenn obliged me a few minutes later by bringing in a hand mirror and holding it out to me as if warding off a vampire. I inhaled painfully. That was not me. It was a creature with a head the shape of a pumpkin, eyelids like clamshells, bruised and puckering lips.

I had gone from showoff to clown, from daredevil to freak. And I had learned a new fear.

*A sundance lodge near Meadow Lake
with a Mountie in the middle, 1909.*
(FRANK CREAN PHOTO)

OUT *of* PLACE

I built up a long list of fears over time: bees, large dogs, horses, bears, hypodermic needles, bombs, Mrs. Carter, God. There were stories behind each of these terrors. Bees because of the hornet stings; dogs because Uncle Eddy's yellow Lab, Butch, had snapped at me and taken a chunk out of my lip; horses because I had seen a stallion kick the boards out of a corral at Marlon and Wade's place; bears and needles because everyone was afraid of them; Mrs. Carter because of the carrot; God because—well, because I was raised Catholic.

Bombs were probably my most justified fear, given the continuing escalations of the Cold War. I was vaguely aware of the arms race and its potential consequences, through news reports and popular post-apocalyptic science fiction shows and novels. But in addition to the generalized Cold War dread of nuclear annihilation and my knowledge that Cold Lake would be vapourized in a first strike, I heard and felt *real* bombs every summer. Our cabin at Jeannette Lake was only a few miles from the eastern edge of the Primrose Lake Air Weapons Range, which was—and is—a training site for NATO bombing missions.

Sometimes we saw the jets streaking across the north-western horizon, or heard the oddly disconnected, direction-less roar of the engines. Once when Glenn and I were fishing on the far side of the lake, an F-18 appeared just above the treetops, not 200 yards away. It was utterly silent, and we were so surprised that we both stood up in the canoe, poised to jump overboard, to seek cover. For a second I thought it might be a Soviet plane, the first wave of an invasion. The NATO pilots weren't supposed to fly outside the boundaries of the bombing range, and certainly not so low. When I recognized the tiny American flag beneath the cockpit, it was only a minor relief. No matter whose side it was on, this thing was bristling with danger. The massive bombs clung to the fuselage like parasites, jutting out in front of the wings.

As we stood there in the wobbly canoe, the plane flew silently out over the water and then banked sharply to the right, fully displaying its malevolent, arrowhead shape. Thinking back, it seems like no coincidence that F-18s are called Hornets. It was as if someone had designed this plane specifically to terrify me. Inside I could see the insectlike form of the pilot, with his helmet and face mask and strangely mandibular, quick-moving arms. Before we had even said a word, its afterburners flashed with a pink glow like a car's cigarette lighter, and it disappeared over the tree-tops on the far side of the bay. We were left with the belated thunder of the engines.

That's how it was: always by surprise, always when you had just forgotten that the planes and bombs existed, when you were napping in a lawn chair or bouncing a yellowtail jig along the bottom of the lake or wading in for a swim. The unpredictability magnified our unease. We flinched at the sight of loons and swallows in the air.

Far more common than close-up sightings of the planes was the sound of the bombs. Most of the time they used "dummy" bombs made of lead or cast iron, which we couldn't hear from the cabin, but several times a year they practised with live ordnance. Sometimes the explosions were almost indistinguishable from thunder, but if the targets were closer to our end of the bombing range, the effect was far more jarring. They sent shock waves through the sand that were like brief earthquakes. The cabin would heave and shudder momentarily, or the beach would shimmy beneath us. It was as if the ground had been changed into muskeg for a second.

The noise would hit an instant later: a thick, heavy sound, not at all like a gunshot. It seemed to come from deep in the earth. Then there would be a moment of absolute silence, like after the firing of the cannons on Remembrance Day. Soon came the other sounds: dogs whining, children crying, men swearing, parents offering words of comfort. Sometimes people had to talk their dogs out from underneath the crawl spaces below their cabins. One of the neighbour kids was so terrified by the bombs that he became almost catatonic. He would fall to the ground clutching his ears and stay there in a heap until his parents came to get him.

I wasn't as frightened as that. Sometimes I even thought the bombs were funny, like the time when Mom stepped into the outhouse and a few seconds later a whole planeload of ordnance exploded in the distance, shaking the cabin. Mom herself didn't find this so amusing.

I never worried that the bombs would accidentally hit us. I was simply shocked by their existence at all—their interruptiveness, their incongruity in this place where we went barefoot for weeks on end, and threw ourselves into the water a dozen times a day, and hiked out to the secret berry patch to pick raspberries or blueberries or pin cherries straight into our mouths. That this should also be the site of bombs and warplanes was hardly comprehensible. Every time we heard the bombs it was a reminder that something was wrong, something was out of place in the world. Either those planes didn't belong or we didn't. It was impossible that the two realities could coexist in the same place.

I also had another fear, a secret one. I never mentioned it to anyone, even though I felt it in my stomach every time I stepped outside the boundary of our yard. I was afraid of Native people. Not so much the women, and certainly not the girls, but the men and especially the boys. They were the most visible. There were always a few Native men standing outside the Stampede Hotel and the Empire and the Hub Café in their plaid shirts and jeans, smoking roll-your-own cigarettes or chewing Copenhagen. Many had braids, but some had flat-top brush cuts, and others kept their hair hidden under their caps. We also saw them in Pete's Billiards Room and Dickowicky's Modern Billiards, where we went to play pinball and Space Invaders and Defender. They talked among themselves, and laughed often, but always quietly. They never spoke to me and they certainly never made any menacing gestures toward me. They rarely even looked in my direction. But still I felt vaguely threatened by them, though

I didn't know exactly why. They were different, they seemed to set themselves apart, and I suppose that was enough. That and the stories about tomahawks and scalping and eyes pinned open in the sun.

Of course it wasn't entirely their own decision to be set apart, though I didn't realize this at the time. I didn't know that for many years the people of Flying Dust were required to get the Indian agent's permission to leave the reserve for any reason. I didn't understand the function of the residential schools. If I had looked more closely I would have seen that the Cree people on the street corners often had a sheepishness about them, which had probably been learned through generations of discrimination. It was as if they *expected* to be denigrated, perhaps even to be feared. This was probably why they seemed to talk only among themselves. It was the solidarity of the oppressed, and it led to a kind of voluntary segregation of the streets: the Native people stood and visited while everyone else walked by them as if they weren't even there. This separation extended to the church, where the Natives always took the pews at the back, as if intuiting their place in the town's social hierarchy. The beer halls in town were surprisingly like the churches: the Indians sitting at the back, in the corners, the most poorly lit places. Even the buses were the same. Maybe they chose to do this, but something must have governed that choice, something must have made them feel they belonged only on the perimeter of these gathering places.

I took that separation for granted when I was a kid. I didn't wonder where it had come from, how it had developed. I didn't think about the exceptions: my friends Gilbert and

Jimmy, and Mrs. Bear, who went to our church and was famous for her beaded mitts and mukluks. There were also Native men who golfed at the course in town and who seemed to be accepted in the clubhouse. But on the streets and in the bars and churches, the separation was largely maintained. And I suppose that division was what reinforced my fear of them. I knew the Native people were different from me, but it was more alarming to recognize that *I* was different from them. They made me feel uneasy, like I didn't belong in my own hometown.

It's clear to me now that there was a vast history to my fear, one that began generations before my birth and that I would not become aware of for many years. It was built on stereotypes of savages and heathens that dated back to a time when Meadow Lake was known only as Paskwâw Sâkâhikan. The whole western culture has always been afraid of Indians, at the same time as it has cheated them and infantilized them and distorted them into jokes and caricatures. I think that simply by being who they were, aboriginals made everyone else question their own belonging, and that questioning tended to raise the most fundamental kinds of fears and insecurities.

I absorbed those fears unconsciously and began to enact them, to give them my own personal reality. I had, after all, like almost every kid of my generation, played cowboys and Indians. I loved *Gunsmoke*. I had heard, and sometimes repeated, the stories about Indian givers, drunk Indians, stupid Indians, lazy Indians, thieving Indians, dead Indians. No aboriginal man had ever threatened me, but I'd heard about the fights in the bars, the number of Native people in jail, the terrible living conditions on some of the reserves. That was all the threat I needed

With the Native boys it was somewhat different because I knew them from school. They weren't just silent presences on the sidewalks but individuals who knew my name and who had good reasons to resent my place in the community. Everything about my relationship with them was conditioned by the environment at school, where I was often favoured and usually the Native kids were not. I was hardly aware of the racism in school because I wasn't the one singled out for mistreatment. But boys like Clayton Matchee were, and Gilbert Lachance, and Kenny Laliberte, and my friend Jimmy Sinclair. I remember that Clayton got in trouble with the teachers regularly, but not for anything substantially different than what other boys did. He was only a low-grade troublemaker—a prankster, a teaser of girls, a kid who got into tussles at recess—yet it seemed he was punished more often and more severely than some of the white boys who got into more serious trouble. At the time I didn't question it much; I still believed that everyone got what they deserved. Even in grade one when Mrs. Goodman took Gilbert up to the front of the class, pulled down his pants, and paddled his ass with a yardstick in front of us all, I didn't think her unfairness had anything to do with Gilbert being Indian. I just thought it was strange and arbitrary that she should humiliate him this way for such a minor transgression as playing soccer with the grade sixes. She didn't know that he would later be welcomed among the white kids because of the very thing she had punished him for: his skill at sports.

Some of the teachers had obvious prejudices, but the racism in my school was even more visible among the kids. As usual, they were less subtle about it than the adults, less aware that there might be anything wrong with what they were doing. I wish I could say I wasn't involved in it, but that would be a lie. I was racist too. I took part in the name-calling, the jokes, the exclusion. I felt it was my natural place to be respected by the teachers and by my peers, but when anyone else was treated unfairly, I didn't come to their aid.

The white boys taunted the Native girls mercilessly, even though most of these girls did their best to remain inconspicuous. I remember Melody Kahpeepitow, with her ill-fitting glasses and stringy hair and perpetual shy half-smile that was offered to the world as a sign of supplication, a plea for treatment less cruel than what she expected. She said nothing in class and kept to herself at noon hour, chewing her balogna sandwiches and paging through the teacher's collection of *Tintin* cartoons, but still somehow she attracted the attention of Darcy Carlson, the class jock. "Melody, you black thing," he would say to her almost offhandedly, with a snarl of emphasis on the last word. "What're you doing by my desk, you black thing, you?" She never answered him, but she flushed sometimes, and her face took on a faraway expression, the classic if-I-ignore-him-he'll-leave-me-alone look. The rest of us gazed on, wondering if she would ever say anything. But she didn't.

The Native boys were taunted too, but usually at more of a distance, and more obliquely: name-calling across the hallways, jokes at the back of the classroom. These boys could be expected to fight back, and they were known to be good at it.

The cleverest tormentors stood near a teacher for protection and whispered their epithets as the Native kids walked by. "Hey, Nitchie. Want some Lysol?" If a fight broke out, the instigator would turn to the teacher with a look of puzzlement. "What? I didn't do anything. . . ."

It was after school and at recess that I understood there were dangers to being white, if you were caught in the wrong situation. In the elementary grades, a boy named Billy Tootoosis used to follow me and my friend Andrew every day after school. I'm not sure Billy understood why he hated us, but he knew I was scared, and I suppose that was good enough for him. He used to come up beside me on the sidewalk and inflate his bony chest and squint at me through the convex lenses of his old-fashioned black-framed glasses. "Wanna fight," he would say. It was a command, not a question. Every time he said it I answered, "I'm your *friend*, Billy." And every time, he accepted this stupid assertion— not because he believed it, but because his question had served its purpose.

I never did fight Billy, but sometimes Andrew did. During their struggles on the lawn of the boulevard, I feigned impartiality by holding their glasses for them. I remember looking down on their fights with one pair of glasses in each hand, like some myopic statue of justice—a self-appointed referee of the battle between the races. As if I could opt out of the battle myself whenever it was convenient.

I didn't always find the neutral ground so easily. There were many other dangerous places in my neighbourhood, many other people to avoid. The Fiddler boys frightened me the most. They travelled together in a little gang, and I often saw them lurking near the T. C. Confectionery or hanging out in the labyrinthine hallways of the hockey rink. Once, when I was in grade one or two, they chased me halfway across town, from the old hospital down to the low-rental housing units and out toward the stampede grounds. They had managed to position themselves between me and home, so there was nothing for me to do but run farther and farther into dangerous territory. I remember glancing from one strange and decrepit house to the next, wondering which of them might contain someone who would protect me. But I believed none of them would.

I kept running. I heard the Fiddler boys laughing as they followed, and sometimes shouting phrases in Cree. The silver jackknife in my front pocket bounced against my leg as I ran, and I remember resolving to use it when the time came. I almost looked forward to the confrontation, imagining the looks on their faces when I waved the blade in the sunlight.

But then, miraculously, the time didn't come. They must have grown bored with the pursuit, because they stopped running and eventually turned down another street.

At the time, I didn't wonder why they had been chasing me in the first place. It seemed inevitable that they would. I wonder now if it wasn't just my fear that made them want to do it. I was never good at disguising fright. I always believed that I could make myself look tough by squinting my eyes and breathing through clenched teeth, but it never worked. I don't suppose the Fiddler boys thought much about why they pursued me either, but if anyone had asked them they might have said it was fun to put a scare into wimpy little white boys. They always gave up the chase before catching me. I suppose to them I was just a bit of entertainment, a sideshow: *let's watch the white kid run!* I think they might even have said I deserved a bit of a scare. I had been blessed with all kinds of things that they were excluded from: relative wealth, the respect of teachers, an expectation in the community that I would make something of myself. And I took it all for granted. I can see how blithely annoying I must have been.

It was all about belonging for them too, I think. In Meadow Lake, belonging was written on our skin. We all shared a knowledge of the difference between brown faces and white, knowledge that came complete with a whole series of lessons in racism: rules about whom we could associate with, where we could feel safe, what we could become when we grew up. Everyone lived by those rules. I knew I belonged in school and in our backyard, whereas theirs was the kingdom of the roadways, the stampede grounds, the reserve. We all patrolled our territories, watching for each other.

Cattle at the Evans Ranch, 1909.
(FRANK CREAN PHOTO)

LEONARD'S RANCH

In the farm and ranch country around Meadow Lake, belonging was less complicated than in town. Despite the profusion of No Trespassing signs on the road allowances, I felt like a visitor rather than a trespasser whenever we roamed the countryside. This was our commonest pastime. Someday Mom and Dad wanted to have a farm of our own, but until then we were weekend pastoralists, driving the dirt roads and open fields and forest trails around home. Ranches were my favourite rambling places because we could wander through them without worrying about ruining anyone's crops, and because they had more variety of wildlife. Around any corner we might see prairie lilies, lady's slippers, a deer, a coyote, a family of partridges. It seemed there was little difference between ranchland and wilderness.

We did much of our wandering in a place called Leonard's Ranch, owned by Leonard Evans, whom Dad had befriended when he first arrived in Meadow Lake. Leonard's grandfather Pete Evans was the first rancher in the area, having moved there with his family in 1908, seeking escape from the influx of new settlers near their previous ranch west of

Battleford. Just before Pete died in 1930, his son Jimmy took over the cattle operation and built it into a thriving business. By the time it became Leonard's Ranch in the mid-fifties, it had grown to nearly the size of a township: twenty-two quarter sections strewn along the Meadow River north of the reserve. Most of it was light sandy soil unsuitable for growing crops, but there was plenty of grass for grazing, and the floodplain of the river provided fertile hay meadows. Leonard had so many cattle and so much land to cover that he often checked on the animals by airplane. It was easier to find them from the air, since they huddled in the forest to protect themselves from insects, and possibly from wolves too.

Despite his use of the airplane, Leonard was not a technology man. He preferred to ride horses much of the time, and he always kept several of them stabled in a large corral near his father's first house, built in 1928. The Evanses had moved into town in the late thirties, but they continued to use the ranch house as a part-time dwelling, and when we first saw it Leonard still lived there occasionally. It was the only old house in the area that looked authentically western to me—looked like it could have come out of a movie. Other homestead log houses that I had seen were rotten and falling down, but this one still had a good roof and unbroken windows and rustic poplar-bough furniture on the front stoop. It was painted red with white trim, and there were half a dozen racks of bleached antlers nailed to the front wall.

The most perilous thing about Leonard's ranch was getting there, across the Meadow River. In the early years there was one bridge at each end of the ranch, and both were unbelievably decrepit. To cross them was an exercise in faith, something like walking on water. The authorities had long ago stopped maintaining these bridges, since they only led to one man's property, and Leonard's efforts at makeshift maintenance—heroic though they were—couldn't keep up to the natural processes of decay and collapse.

We crossed the nearest bridge hundreds of times, each time with greater trepidation. Its pilings had heaved and swayed with so many seasons of ice-out and spring flooding that the bridge deck was bowed and twisted into hills and valleys. Driving across it was like riding on the back of a whale. It arched and plunged in great ponderous waves, and you never knew when it was going to head straight for the depths.

It got noticeably worse every season. Each spring the peaks of the corrugated surface were higher and the valleys were lower than we had remembered. On the upstream side, a gigantic nest of logs and branches and floating garbage continually built up against the soggy pilings. By the time I was ten, it had become such a dense thicket of detritus that I wondered how the river flowed through it at all. By then there were several boulder-sized holes in the desiccated wood of the deck, and Leonard had tried to solve this problem by nailing three rows of two-by-sixes like a set of train tracks across the bridge. If we slipped off those narrow rails, we would very likely punch a hole in the brittle wood and—if we were *lucky*—the truck would be stuck there. My only solace was that if the truck ever did fall through, we would probably land on the logjam below us.

Though the bridge terrified us, it was also one of the biggest attractions of Leonard's Ranch. We cringed about it for miles before we got there, and we always double-checked our preparations to be sure that our windows were rolled down, our doors unlocked, our seat belts disconnected, before Dad inched us tentatively onto the row of two-by-sixes that undulated across to the far side. When the front wheels first touched the bridge, we inhaled vastly and noisily and then held the air in, pinching our noses.

It was one of the only times in his life when Dad drove excruciatingly slowly.

"Step on it, Dad!" we gasped, and then quickly inhaled again. But he didn't step on it. He crouched over the steering wheel like our neighbour Mrs. Tiefenbach, pretending to be obsessed with safety as he navigated our way across the pot-holed surface. Glenn and Michelle and I stared out the window at the holes—some of which gave views of water below—and at the laughably feeble railing that swayed along beside us, and at the jutting tree branches that protruded from beneath the bridge. We crawled along, our eyes bulging, our clenched lips turning blue. When the Jeep clunked down on the far bank, we hyperventilated with joy and gave cheers for our own audacity. Another miraculous passage!

The bridge at the far end, down by our favourite fishing hole, was in even worse shape, and I don't remember ever driving across it, though Mom and Dad assured me that we had. Its peaks and valleys were mountainous, and there were basketball-sized holes in the wood, as if it had been a target of aerial bombardment. Even to walk on it required serious nerve. But we did walk on it many times, because it was only twenty feet upstream from the best pickerel hole. Whenever the bank got crowded, Glenn and I would climb up onto the structure and cast down to the good spot. Landing a fish from up there was more of a challenge, but sometimes we could swing the fish like a pendulum until Mom or Dad grabbed it from shore and removed the hook.

In 1975 a flood washed away the road on both sides of the far bridge, and after that, the structure was stranded out in the middle of the stream, draped in dead weeds and grasses, looking like a wrecked galleon. Two or three years later there was another flood and the bridge broke apart, sending its separate pieces down the river. When the water receded that year, the only sign of the bridge was a small mound of wood, like a dishevelled beaver lodge, in the middle of the stream. By this time a new bridge was built half a mile downstream, on a new road that went straight north from the sawmill instead of meandering through Leonard's Ranch. Many people travelled this new road, and suddenly our fishing hole by the old bridge was no longer a secret. Dozens of people crowded the banks each spring, and within a few years the fish disappeared.

But anyway there was something at Leonard's Ranch I liked even more than fishing: archaeology. Leonard had found dozens of arrowheads and spear points and stone hammers on his land, and he kept them all in large cardboard boxes in his Meadow Lake house. Dad took Glenn and me over there to see them once. I had seen arrowheads in museums, but always they were under glass, and labelled with scientific names. In Leonard's collection they were in open boxes, which he pulled down from a shelf so we could reach in and touch them, turn them over, feel the serrated edges of the flint, the quartzite, the obsidian. I was amazed by the variety of the colours. Many of them were pastel shades, almost pink, almost ultramarine.

"That's quite the thing," Dad said, holding a bulbous pink spear point in his palm. "Could bring down an elk with that, I bet."

As far as I knew, Leonard had not read up on the artifacts, and his collection was not organized by any noticeable rationale, but still he treated them with extraordinary respect. He searched through the boxes to find the most unusual ones—the tiny obsidian wedges, the larger pink and bluish ones with delicate notches at their bases, the ungainly, top-heavy, rounded spear points. There were also two oblong stone hammers and a hide scraper made of deer antler, which he scraped against his open palm to demonstrate its use.

"They never wasted anything, those people," he said.

We asked how he had found so many of them.

"Oh, my dad and my grandpa found lots before me, but I found a fair number over the years. Never went out looking for them. I just learned to keep my eye out, specially when I'm on horseback, because you don't want your horse stepping on one of these." He ran a finger along the edge of a large spear point. "Cripple a horse, or a steer too. So you keep one eye on the ground, and every once in a while you see something there in the sand, especially down by the river. They must have hunted more down there; it makes sense, I guess. They were quite the hunters when you think, all they had was a little piece of stone on the end of a stick."

The arrowheads made me think of ancient civilizations like the ones depicted in *National Geographic* articles with titles like "A Lost Culture" or "A Vanished People." But of course these people hadn't vanished. Leonard and his father and grandfather would have had regular contact with the

Cree people from Flying Dust, which was only a few miles downstream of the ranch. It is likely that the Natives continued to hunt on the ranchland for a time after Pete Evans took possession of it, and that they did so with his blessing. Boundaries were not so strict in the early days of settlement, before barbed wire was available. The Native people were sometimes even looked upon as neighbours in those early years, rather than as a threatening presence. Goods were traded, gifts were sometimes exchanged. Some pioneers were even invited to the powwow ceremonies at Flying Dust, where they experienced first-hand the mesmeric power of Cree dance and song.

After seeing Leonard's collection of arrowheads, Glenn and Michelle and I became obsessed with the possibility of finding some there ourselves. We walked up and down the roadways and cattle trails, kicking at the sand, overturning logs, reaching down gopher holes. We even held archaeological digs. The first one was near the end of the winding ranch road, along a high bank about a hundred feet above the floodplain of the river. There were four long parallel lines in the soil there at the edge of the hill. Dad told us these shallow depressions were all that was left of the trenches that a Native band had dug to defend themselves from attackers. I had never heard of Crees digging trenches, but Dad's speculation made a certain amount of sense: the high hillside was a natural fortification, a perfect place to protect oneself from enemies. It also offered proximity to the river for both food and transportation, and a clear view of the surrounding valley. With Dad's encouragement, we imagined great battles being staged on that hillside, with the inhabitants of the hill dug into their trenches, firing waves of arrows down into the advancing ranks of their enemies. I wondered who these enemies might have been: Other Indians? Or maybe soldiers like in the 1885 rebellion? Dad didn't say. His vision of the trenches was probably more inspired by World War I history than by anything in real Cree history, but still it was plausible enough to us. These battles, Dad said, were what explained the presence of all the arrowheads on the land.

We centred our dig at the edge of one of the trenches. Dad and Glenn and I took turns with the spade, carefully lifting out each clump of sand, which the others sifted through with their bare hands. We dug down at least three feet, in four separate places, but all we ever found was small stones, roots, pine cones, and chunks of dried cow pie. I didn't mind particularly. We were at least making trenches, just like the imagined Indians. I jumped into one thigh-deep hole and tried to huddle down, like people in gunfights did on TV, and I peered down the steep bank toward the river in search of enemies. I wondered if any of the Indians had been killed in this trench, or buried there.

"Time to fill it back in," Dad said. "We're skunked."

But we did find a stone hammer near that same spot a few years later, along with the skeleton of what looked like a caribou. The strange, clublike antlers were what attracted us to the site in the first place. We had scrambled down the steep bank with its row of trenches to the edge of the floodplain, with the intention of having a wiener roast down there, out of the wind, when Glenn noticed a strangely shaped piece of wood sticking two or three inches out of the ground.

"Hey," he said. "Driftwood!"

It took surprisingly little digging to push away the sand and unearth the antlers, which were still attached to a long, jawless skull with a pointy nose.

"Well I'll be," Dad said, brushing the sand off the antlers, poking a finger through the eyeholes so clumps of dirt fell down from the brain cavity onto his shoes. "What do you think this is, Buzz?"

We were only slightly disappointed to learn that it was a caribou rather than a duckbilled dinosaur. Dad told us that the woodland caribou used to live as far south as the Height of Land, before the settlers came and cut down the trees and planted crops. When the wheat and barley flourished, the white-tailed deer moved northward to feed on it and crowded out the habitat of the caribou. This was long before any of us had arrived there. Dad had never seen a live caribou anywhere near Meadow Lake.

Of course, the discovery of the antlers and skull was enough to renew our enthusiasm for digging. It was getting late, but we stayed after the wiener roast to poke at the ground with our hands, with sticks, with the heels of our shoes. We hadn't brought a shovel or even an axe. We didn't really expect to find anything more, given our previous failures, but we surprised ourselves by unearthing a ring of fire-blackened rocks not far from the caribou. And a little farther away, Dad found another oblong stone that didn't have the dark markings and cracks that the fire rocks had.

"See here," Dad said. "See? You know what this is?"

He ran his index finger along a shallow ridge that circumscribed the rock. It looked almost like an accident of geology, but the ring was a little too regular for that.

"Remember the ones Leonard showed us?" Dad picked up a stick that Glenn had been using for digging. "You tie it on with a piece of leather," he said, "and it's a hammer. They used these to crush the bones of the animals, to get at the marrow."

He swung the makeshift assembly and the head of the hammer thumped into the sand. It didn't look as hammer-like as the ones Leonard had found, but still it might have been one of them.

"Just imagine the people who used this hammer," he said. "Before this place was Leonard's Ranch, there might have been teepees all along the river, and birchbark canoes, and racks for drying fish."

It was an idyllic life, the way I pictured it: in summer, with smoke rising from a row of teepees and strips of pickerel drying on a rack and moose skins curing beside a smudge fire. It was a hopelessly idealized image, drawn largely from the books I had read on Native customs in grade four, which were invariably illustrated with pastoral scenes of indigenous communities. It's unfortunate that I didn't make the connection between these romanticized ancestors and the Native people of present-day Meadow Lake, whom I still feared. But despite my persisting illusions, I learned something important that day. I was struck by how quickly things had changed here in the years since my dad was born. What other animals had inhabited this land, had drunk from the edge of this river, only a generation or two earlier? And what people had passed through here, and lived here, looking out on this magnificent valley with the stands of poplar trees in the far distance, smelling the grass and the sage in the air? It was the first occasion when I realized that the land is deep in time, that it is full of other lives, other stories, other presences. The earliest settlers on this land arrived in 1908, but before that there had been Native people here for dozens and dozens of generations. It was as if the homesteaders were only the finest layer of dust covering the immense hill at our backs, and underneath was a mountain of unspoken stories.

I kept one of the great branching caribou antlers to show my friends, but before we went home, we put the stone hammer and the fire rocks back in the ground where we had found them. "They don't belong to us," Dad said, and it felt right to leave them there. Over the seasons the soil has covered them back up, and in my more recent visits I haven't been able to find them.

I think now that the steep hill, with the bones and the hammer and the fire ring at its base, might have been a buffalo jump, like the ones I have seen in southeastern Alberta. There were never as many buffalo in the north as on the southern plains, but they were still relatively common there at the end of the nineteenth century. When Chief Gregoire Matchee was an old man, he remembered hunting buffalo in earlier days, before the settlers came. The Crees would ride up beside the stampeding animals, lean over, and stab them with long knives. At the age of seven he had killed a buffalo calf in this manner, thus earning the name Maĉi, which means "the hunter."

Before Chief Matchee's ancestors had horses, it is likely that they would have used whatever hunting methods were available to them, including the buffalo jump, wherever the shape of the land made it possible. And of course elk and caribou could have been herded over the precipice too. The rows of trenches might have been put there to trip the animals so they couldn't stop themselves before the edge. I imagine the people of the hill crouching there at the bottom, stone hammers and spears in hand, waiting for the herd of driven caribou to come thundering over the edge. The land becoming a weapon.

After the stone hammer find, I was so fascinated with the prehistory of the place that I even took time out from fishing at the bridge to wander up on that hill and look for arrowheads. I would choose a spot and then kneel down and sift through the fine, dusty sand with my bare hands. I always found plenty of small rocks, many of them the same colour as the arrowheads and spear points that Leonard had found, but none of them looked at all convincing as projectile points.

Once when I was about fourteen, I took my cousin Gordy up the hill while our families were fishing. I had told him all about the stone hammer, and he was sure we could find more artifacts.

"Watch out for bears," Dad said as Gordy and I walked off with the spade. Dad and Uncle Art had scared some of us once by crashing through the bush, growling, when we were digging for artifacts. I didn't think this reminder was particularly amusing. We would show Dad this time: we would come back with an arrowhead.

And we did. It took us a long time, digging and filling in our holes, sifting through them and picking out the likely-looking stones. After more than an hour, we had found several good-looking stones, but none of them were arrowheads. It was getting late.

"Hey," Gordy said, holding up one of the stones, a reddish one that was vaguely triangular. "This one might do."

And he put it down on the flat face of the spade and began chipping away at it with a larger rock. Edges crumbled, flecks of stone broke away. I could hardly believe it was working, but yes, I could see the shape emerging, the ridges coming to a definite point. I imagined Gordy and me wearing buckskin and feathers, preparing ourselves for the hunt, speaking softly in Cree.

"*Tansi nîstâw,*" I said, exhausting half my vocabulary in the language.

"Tuktoyaktuk," he answered.

In a few minutes he had fashioned a reasonable facsimile of an arrowhead—somewhat off-kilter and lacking the notches at the base, but still, it looked like a very old one, one that had been damaged over the years.

"Not bad, eh?" he said.

We marched back down the hill and I showed it to Dad, who was just packing up his fishing rod and tackle box.

"Let's see." He squinted, lifting it from my palm where I was carefully trying to display its most authentic-looking profile. He turned it over, rubbed his finger against the roughened edges.

"Well I'll be," he said. "Chas, have a look here. The boys finally found an arrowhead." He held it up to the light for Uncle Charlie to see.

This was probably the only time I ever succeeded in pulling one over on Dad, and I was alarmed by the ease with which we had done it. I knew he was about to begin some speculation about the hunter who had made this arrowhead and what he had used the arrow for—and I couldn't stand the thought of it. Seeing him so perfectly deceived was too much.

"Pretty good, eh?" I said to Uncle Charlie. "We made it."

"Really. Little Indians, are you?"

"Yep."

I got Gordy's elbow in my ribs. "Come on! We had him going."

"Looks pretty authentic to me," Dad said. "Guess you better take it back where you found it."

"But—"

"Just be sure it's dug down good and deep so no heifer steps on it," he added, and turned back toward the truck.

"Jeez," Gordy said. "It's mine."

But without further argument, we climbed back up the hill and carefully placed the arrowhead in one of the holes we had dug. Years later, when I insisted to Dad that Gordy and I had made that arrowhead, he still refused to believe me.

The farm.

SECOND HOME

After several years of dreaming about country life, we finally did move, in the summer of 1976, to a farm three miles from the edge of town. It didn't feel like a momentous event at the time—just a change to a larger house, where I could have my own bedroom, and a much bigger yard to play in. Many things stayed the same. The Height of Land still flashed its enigmatic messages down on us every night, and my various fears stayed with me, and we still went into town almost every day, for school, or shopping, or church, or to visit friends. But when I look back now, I can see that the farm was a revelation. Michelle and Glenn and I had twenty acres of bush to trudge through, and a pasture for horses, and a real barn with a hayloft to climb in. There was no end to the possibilities for exploration, and we dedicated ourselves to experiencing all of it, in every season. Over the coming years I came to know that place more intimately than anywhere I have ever been.

It was an elemental life. We learned to appreciate the minutest progress of the seasons by watching the growth and eventual death of the plants, the movements of the sun on the horizon, the smells in the air. In late August the most delicious aromas drifted past us from the ripened fields: smells of rust and humus, with already a hint of the smokiness of autumn. In February the snow crystals changed their shape to become like salt or sugar, heavy and less delicate than before, but gleaming with new geometry, and giving off an unmistakable smell that was halfway between peppermint and peppercorn. There were always tiny specks of dirt that looked like ground pepper in snow, if you studied it closely enough, as we often did before we licked it out of the palms of our mitts. We were inveterate snow eaters. We liked the late-winter snow the best, for its flavour as well as its aroma, not to mention the fact that it contained more water. The soft, powdery snow of November was all cold and little moisture—not worth the numbing of your tongue.

We came to know the place by feeding on it, absorbing it into ourselves. In early June there were wild strawberries hiding in the long grass by the highway, and we would go out there with teacups or tiny Tupperware bowls, or simply with an open palm to pick into. We had to get right down on our knees and reach under the leaves for the minuscule berries, no bigger than a pea. Once in a while we would get enough for Mom to make a small flan or a biscuit dessert, but most of the time we simply devoured the berries at the end of our picking sessions: two or three glorious mouthfuls of that astonishing flavour, at once delicate, syrupy, and explosive.

After the strawberries there were wild raspberries, dewberries, and chokecherries, all of which grew in the garden or in the bush around the house. Not far away we could pick saskatoons and pin cherries and blueberries. We foraged all summer long, if not on wild fruit then on rhubarb pulled from the garden or dried wheat straight from the granary, which we chewed and chewed until it became a soft bland gum. In the fall we picked wild rosehips, bit them apart, tossed aside the furry seeds, and ate the leathery skin with its rich red paste on the underside.

To be there was to always have our senses full. Even in the seeming barrenness of winter we would see tracks of unidentified creatures in the snow, or rows of puffed-up chickadees on the tree branches, or simply the spectacle of the hoarfrost encrusting everything with fragile ornamentation. In summer we were dazzled by the canola in bloom: a swatch of buttercup yellow, a quarter section of sunlight. After the bloom it had a musty, rank smell for a few weeks as the pods started to mature. Shortly after that, in late August, there was the magnificent bronzing of the barley field as it changed from green to ripened brown.

"The barley's turning," we would say.

"Starting to turn, all right. Wheat'll be ready soon too."

And always there was the sky. Out on the farm it was even more immense and more sharply focused than in town. In the daytime we could see the shadows of clouds moving across the fields toward or away from us. We could watch the grey streaks of a hailstorm unleashing itself on our neighbour's crop or perhaps on a field two townships away. At night, the sky was so clear it had depth; you could tell that some stars were more distant than others. The Milky Way was not so milky here, not a wash of light but an infinitely complex pattern of individual stars. It's no accident that I became fascinated with space at that time. I consulted star charts, memorized the names of constellations, plotted the movements of planets. I asked for a telescope for my thirteenth birthday and used it to study the puzzling, puckered face of the Moon. Sometimes, with a special attachment, I used my telescope to examine the sun, with its freckling of dark sunspots, each of them storms of radiation several Earths across.

I was captivated by the earthly effects of those sun storms: the northern lights that regularly draped themselves over the sky. They were usually a ghostly green, but often also pink, and sometimes a mixture of the two. I have since learned that there are few places in the hemisphere that are visited as often by these ethereal shows. To me it was natural to see them not only hanging there in the northern distance but also swinging and dancing directly overhead, and sometimes even to the south of us, shimmering above the Height of Land. They pulsed in and out of existence, sometimes disappearing altogether for several seconds and then reappearing instantly in their full brilliance. Dad had told us we could call the northern lights down to us if we whistled at exactly the right pitch, so some nights we stood in the barnyard, leaning our heads as far back as possible, and tried to whistle. Sometimes the wavering swags of light seemed to sway, genii-like, in response.

Living on a farm, we also witnessed many other displays of the "wonders" of life and death—though mostly it was death that we saw, death at our own hands or at the whims of the climate, of disease, of predation. There were numerous litters of kittens, and we were shocked to watch the process of their birth:

"She's pooping kittens mom!"

"Eeeeuuucchh."

"They look like snakes. Snakes without eyes."

But we also saw what happened later, when some of them died of distemper, others were killed on the highway, and many simply disappeared. When one litter of particularly cute Siamese-like kittens vanished, we followed the frantic mother cat up to the hayloft. Mom later told us that the tomcat must have come back and killed them. All we saw was the five tiny heads, their eyes still sealed shut, their blonde fur unmarked by the carnage. We didn't speak as we looked at them arrayed there on the straw like something from *Friday the Thirteenth* or *Hallowe'en*. What, we wondered, could do something like this?

Our dogs also disappeared at an alarming rate, mostly because of the highway. Some were killed by cars, but others must have just wandered away, or maybe people picked them up along the road and took them home. Then there was our asthmatic horse, Sparky, who for years had suffered from a kind of whooping cough: a slow, rhythmic spasm of rasping breath, often accompanied by explosive farts. The vet had told us this wasn't serious, but it was. Sparky died on Michelle's ninth birthday, and Michelle was the one who discovered the body—along with a dozen of her school friends who were there for the party. No amount of explanation could convince those kids that Sparky was only resting. They *knew*, and some of them were stricken with the knowledge. It was Glenn's job to create a diversion—a treasure hunt—while Dad and I loaded Sparky in the truck and hauled him to the far end of the wheat field. Even that wasn't the end of it. For several years, successive generations of dogs rediscovered the carcass and dragged a few of Sparky's bones back to the house.

On a farm, death can't be avoided. We had heard the agricultural gothic of Dad's farm stories for years, and now we saw that it was true. We knew all about the mess of death, the smells of it, the many surprising variations it could take. There was the leaping, spurting saturnalia of our chicken butchering every fall, and there was the far less dramatic but more singular, more personal, slow wasting of disease, of exposure, sometimes even of old age. Death was a constant presence, and I think we were affected by that, by the physicality of it, even the necessity of it. Being at home there meant coming to terms with the omnipresence of mortality, and understanding that we were often responsible for the lives of the creatures that lived there with us.

We formed a bond with the place almost immediately, but this was not the same thing as being accepted into the rural community. For Glenn and Michelle and me, making that connection was difficult. Everyone knew we weren't *real* farm kids, and we were sometimes teased for this on the school bus. In rural childhood lore, all townies were necessarily wimps, and I knew I wasn't likely to prove that stereotype wrong. My experiences with Marlon and Wade had proved that. I was terrified the other kids would discover my embarrassing ineptitude with pellet guns, motorcycles, tractors. All the farm kids had apparently learned to drive before they were twelve, and most of the boys owned dirt bikes. The most obvious thing about these boys was that they were all utterly fearless. Each of them told me so, repeatedly, and I never thought to challenge their assertions.

The farm itself was a strange world at first, too, though for the most part that strangeness was inviting, exotic. In the garden there were dozens of pumpkin-sized dark glass bulbs with silver coatings on one side and wires sprouting from the hindquarters. We learned that they were broken television tubes, which the former owners, the Honsbergers, had arranged as lawn ornaments. Mr. Honsberger had been a part-time TV repairman as well as a farmer. I thought the blank tubes were beautiful in an otherworldly way, especially when the dew formed on them or the rain streaked down the darkened glass, and I could look at my own misshapen reflection in the distorted surface. In the shop we found the remains of several disembowelled TV cabinets, missing their tubes, and we used to play TV with them. Glenn and Michelle would crawl inside the sets and pretend to be the characters on *Hogan's Heroes* and *Three's Company* and *M*A*S*H*. I was too big to fit inside, so I had to be the director.

It was weird to see signs of other people's presence on the land, even though we knew we weren't the first occupants. The Honsbergers had been there for thirty-six years, and had built the house, the workshop, the barn, the granaries, and the chicken coop. They had planted many of the trees and all of the perennials in our garden. I assumed they had been the original homesteaders, but I learned later that they had purchased the place in 1939 from a man named Cup Warren, who had started his homestead there in the early thirties. I never learned anything else about Cup Warren, but it was somehow comforting to think that our farm had been known as "the Warren place" decades before I was born.

Our awareness of the farm's past came largely through garbage. We practised a kind of freelance archaeology on the refuse mounds near the house and some of the outbuildings, though our approach was less intensive than our digs at Leonard's Ranch. Mostly we wandered in the bush looking for junk that had been thrown back there, hoping to find valuable antiques, or at least some corroded relics of the homestead era. I was particularly fond of old-fashioned beer bottles, and Dad had encouraged me to believe they were virtually priceless. But in our homestead garbage dumps the only recognizable things we found were old tobacco tins and shards of white china and unidentified pieces of rusted metal. Even these seemed like treasures, though Mom wouldn't let us take them in the house because they were so filthy.

"You guys stay outta that crap pile," she would say. "*Feeda*, what a smell."

I had to admit she was right: history stunk, at least in this case. But still we were drawn back to the crap pile again and again, clattering through the leavings of the previous inhabitants, digging past layers of rotten leaves and decayed boards and God knew what else, hoping for that precious discovery that would vindicate our efforts. I wondered what would happen if we got serious about it, if we dug there for days, for weeks. How long would it take to get to the bottom of that garbage—and then what would we find? Arrowheads? Caribou bones?

Of course we had been looking in the wrong places for homestead treasures. The pioneers were famous for never throwing things away; they just set them aside with the intention of fixing them later. We ended up finding the most interesting things arranged neatly beside the shop and the granaries: an old bedspring, a huge steel tractor wheel, a hand-plow, the head of an axe. Our best find was the wrecked car behind the shop, with broken windows and missing seats and poplar trees growing up through the open engine compartment. It seemed almost prehistoric. We climbed inside it sometimes and stood there on the seatless floorboards trying to turn its immense black steering wheel. I imagined how the kids on the bus would look at me if they saw me driving that spectacular rustbucket into town, one arm draped casually out the window.

Inside the shop we found a collection of old tools—a drawknife, a handsaw, a scythe—and in the corner behind the steel-drum stove was the ancient forge: a circular bed of cracked and charred concrete mounted on a steel frame, with a whirring cast-iron bellows that we liked to crank, pretending we were blacksmiths, creating something new out of the scrap heap we'd found outside. I tried to imagine what Mr. Honsberger and Cup Warren must have made there. Perhaps all the other tools? I could hardly guess. Blacksmithing was as unknown to me as alchemy. I knew only that it involved hammering and sweating and plunging glowing metal into buckets of water. Somehow the fire and the water made things stronger.

Those implements reminded me that almost every aspect of homesteading had involved punishing physical labour. It was all about hardship, perseverance. Whatever their delusions may have been, it was clear that the homesteaders had indeed worked slavishly for most of their lives to make a living here, to make a home. I wondered if that was still the case, if there would be some test of belonging that I might have to endure.

We felt nothing like farmers, even though Mom and Dad had both been raised on homesteads and had told us many stories about milking cows, feeding pigs, building stooks, snaring gophers. They had both grown up just after the Depression, when farming was a matter of hard work and luck, when it had little to do with marketing or chemicals or technology. A great deal had changed in the world of agriculture since their youth, and they weren't entirely prepared for the new realities of rural life.

Dad was puzzled by the inner mysteries of machines, and he distrusted them, I think. He had no real interest in working on them, but we were often left with no choice when something broke down at an inopportune time. We spent hours of fruitless labour on the garden tractor, the rototiller, the lawn mower, the chainsaw. Luckily our neighbour Art Waddington came to our rescue whenever something mechanical needed fixing. When it came to carpentry, mending fences, and painting, we were all somewhat capable, though we were far from being experts. What Dad and Mom were particularly good at was growing things. They loved gardening, and they spent most of their time outside, especially in spring and summer. The rest of the business of farming they had to learn as they went along.

That learning would have been much more difficult without the help of the rural community. While the kids on the bus were skeptical about us, their parents must have felt a certain communitarian sympathy for us, because we were welcomed with a hospitality and a generosity that was far beyond what anyone could have expected. The neighbours might have watched us with a certain amount of amusement, pseudo-farmers that we were, but they also shepherded us through the first few years with a seemingly endless supply of volunteer labour. They never gave us lessons about farm life, and they rarely gave advice, even when asked. What they gave was simply help. Our neighbours were there to help us build fences, fix machinery, cut hay, mow lawn, dig a root cellar, break horses, trim the hooves of cattle, dehorn cattle, squeeze warbles out of the cattle's lumpy backs, build new steps on the barn so we could have barn dances, fix the roofs of the granaries, and on and on. They were the kind of people who were there to help before we even knew we needed help. And they did this all without any expectation of gain or even reciprocation. Just for the satisfaction of knowing that something that needed doing had been done. I realize now that this remarkable helpfulness was a remnant of homesteader traditions, carried over from the not-so-distant time when the pioneers had to depend on each other for their lives.

We made our own efforts to learn the ways of modern agriculture, mostly through the 4-H Beef club, which I joined when I was twelve. I didn't realize it was meant to be as much of an education for Mom and Dad as it was for me. I joined because some of my friends were joining, and it meant a few extra days off school for Achievement Day and for our annual field trips. Besides, I'd heard that I would be able to sell my calf at the end of the year for a profit. What I didn't think about was the amount of work it would be. But I learned.

Within the first couple of years I had absorbed all kinds of bovine lore. I knew the names of the cow's four stomachs (rumen, reticulum, omasum, abomasum), and I had memorized all the cuts of meat and the various feeding regimens that would produce a steer ready for market. We took field trips to the Agribition in Regina and to Vetavision in Saskatoon, where I was able to reach through a gaping porthole in the side of a living heifer and feel the churning motions of the masticated slop inside one of her stomachs (it was the reticulum, I believe). I learned how to lead a thousand-pound "beast" (Dad's word) around the show ring with nothing more than a halter rope and a cane. The early training sessions for this skill were terrifying, both for me and for my chosen beast. In the first couple of years, Dad would hold on to the rope behind me so he could haul down the steer if it took off. But when I was fourteen, it was time for me to lead the steer by myself.

Getting an eleven- or twelve-hundred-pound steer to follow a kid around the show ring should be classified as a kind of circus trick, something like training an elephant to stand on one foot. The main difference is that cattle are much stupider than elephants. They have no idea what you want them to do, and even when you show them step by step, they don't usually catch on. The process is one of simple repetition—which is not so simple when the animal weighs fifteen times as much as its supposed master. A steer will stand there in blank confusion, staring swollen-eyed as you pull and strain at the halter rope, and then after three or four minutes of this recalcitrance it will suddenly bolt to the left or the right, or straight ahead, and it will stampede around the corral until it damn well feels like stopping.

And they can kick, too. Not straight backward like horses, but sideways, an ungainly but powerful straight-leg hook that reaches up to about groin level on a fourteen-year-old. Don't ask how I know.

Mom explained to me that Dad was learning about cattle just as I was, but somehow Dad himself never let on to me that he was on a learning curve. He was determined to teach me how to lead that beast, to see me conquer at least one of my fears before I reached adulthood. It was simple, he told me. All you had to do was show him you were the boss, and the only way to do this was to dig in your heels. Dig in your heels and *don't let go*. I heard this advice many times before it came to the actual test. I had pointed out to Dad that he had a great advantage over me in size and strength, but he wouldn't be sidetracked. When the time came, I was going to succeed.

I even believed this myself when we finally got around to that first training session of the year. I had a kind of fatalistic bravado: I would do this or I would die trying.

There were four steers in the corral, and we had been feeding them a fast-gain diet for seven months. The results of that diet were piled up around the corral in a layer about two feet thick. It was late March, an early thaw. The top four inches of the accreted cow shit had melted. This didn't disgust me. The smell of cow shit is actually pleasant, is in fact hardly different from the smell of their food: rich, grassy, vaguely musty. You wonder if their digestive system really *does* anything, despite the four stomachs. Still, shit is shit, and I was prepared for it as well as for the cold, in my rubber boots with felt liners, my winter chore jacket, ski gloves, a tuque. Glenn and Michelle were there to watch me, though I think they were cheering for the steer. I didn't care. They would have their own turns within a couple of years.

We managed to herd my steer into the squeeze chute and slip the halter on him, and then Dad turned him around for me and pulled him out into the middle of the corral. He was a slow one. He held his head down, nearly on the ground, and Dad had to drag him along, step by step, telling me all the while to watch his technique of holding the rope, his method of bracing himself in case the steer should bolt. The three other animals were huddled in the corner, staring at us in bovine horror. Glenn called out, "Make him go fast, Dad!" and I told him to shut up. The steer glared balefully at us, his front legs splayed, his dewlap dangling in the muck, steam blasting rhythmically from his nostrils. Dad let him rest there for a minute, and then he told me to come up and take the rope. I grabbed on behind where he was holding. I wanted the rope to be long so I wouldn't have to get too close to the beast. We transferred the rope with caution, and for a full minute both of us were holding on. Then Dad let go and stepped away. He climbed halfway up the fence and sat there on the top board, like cowboys do at the rodeo.

"Okay," Dad said. "Pull him nice and slow."

I pulled. I leaned back as far as I dared and used my legs, arms, and back to drive as much force onto that rope as I possibly could. The rope stretched out as straight as a guitar string from my hand to the halter. The steer only lowered his head a little more, his eyes rolling partway up into his skull It was like a tug-of-war at school. I had never been on a winning team.

After a while of this deadlock, Dad came up behind the steer and slapped him on the rump. I was ready, but nothing happened. Another slap. A twist of the tail. Slap. Slap. Slap.

There was nothing different about that final slap, but for some reason it set the steer off. It took one swift roundhouse kick at Dad, narrowly missing his right thigh, and then it lurched instantly forward, directly at me.

"DIG—" Dad yelled.

I had been pulling so hard that I stumbled backward. One hand went down in the muck, but I didn't let go of the rope, and I didn't fall. I popped back upright, hands braced in front of me, gripping the rope. Which did no good because the steer was still coming straight for me.

"IN—"

I couldn't back up fast enough to gain tension on the rope. How the hell could a beast so huge and stupid move so quickly? It was all I could do to sidestep that slavering, bulge-eyed, shovel-shaped head as it steamed toward me. The beast stampeded past my left shoulder like a Spanish bull past a matador. Except neither of us was so graceful. It's difficult to be graceful when you're ankle deep in manure.

"YOUR—"

I thought for an instant I was safe, but the steer kept running toward his three dullard compatriots in the corner. When I realized this, there was maybe a foot of slack left in the rope.

"HEELS!"

I swear to God I dug in my heels, just as the rope snapped taut. I dug them in and leaned back and readied myself for the lurch. It would be like doing a jump-start on water skis. Yes. I would ski behind this beast like I had seen steer wrestlers doing at the stampede. Even if I had to dig furrows with my heels, eventually I would slow him down and stop him. Show him who was boss.

I'm proud to say that my grip on the rope never faltered. Other aspects of my plan were less successful. I skied for maybe a few inches, and then my heels hit a piece of submerged frozen dung and I was yanked right off my feet.

I landed on knees and elbows but managed to roll over onto my right side so I could hold my head up high enough to see where I was going. I had no thoughts of letting go or holding on. It was beyond my control now; I was merely a weight at the end of a rope, plowing through a corral full of half-frozen shit. I must have slipped a little farther back on the rope, because I was a few feet behind the steer now. I watched his hind legs pumping, his back seesawing. Bits of muck flew up off his blackened fetlocks as he galloped toward the other steers. When he reached them, he turned to keep running along the fenceline. And they, being herd animals, quickly joined in the stampede.

Now it was serious. I was under one of them, the big tan Charolais. All I saw was stiff bovine legs thrashing all around me, and the flash of white fence posts off to the side. The thunder of hooves against the ice, and the suck and slop of the mud, and the sandpaper sound of their quick-time breathing. Dad and Glenn and Michelle must have been yelling, but I didn't hear them. I was under the steer only for a few seconds but it seemed like much longer. Then my shoulder slammed into something hard on the ground, and the force deflected me out from under the animal. Another one was there but it moved aside for me as if by instinct. For a brief moment, I was part of the herd.

Then they stopped. All of them looked over at Dad, their heads held high, their bellies pulsing for breath.

I stood up. My boots were packed tight with a mixture of straw and snowmelt and shit. My gloves were caked with it too, and the rope was like a long strand of intestine. I was plastered from tuque to heels.

But I hadn't let go. I grinned.

"Why the hell didn't you let go?" Dad said. It was a reprimand, but also a serious question, as if he really wanted to understand why anyone would be so stupid. But somewhere at the back of that question I thought I could detect a measure of pride.

"Couldn't" was all I could say for myself.

Things were different after that. In the spring, after I sold my steer, I took all the money I had made and went directly to the Yamaha dealership in town. I picked out the fastest dirt bike in the place. And for the next five summers, I rode that thing like hell.

Goose hunting.

ORIENTATION

We got to know the surrounding area mostly by rambling—
by going for drives and sometimes boat rides or snowmobile
trips. It had started with our leisurely tours through
Leonard's Ranch and along the berry-picking trails near our
cabin, but it became more elaborate as we got older.
We crisscrossed the grid roads and fields and forests in
the fabled outlying districts—regions I knew only from
seeing their names on the sides of school buses: Bluebell,
Four Corners, Morin Creek, Dunfield, Cabana, Neeb,
Golden Ridge, Resby-Rialto. I loved the sound of those
names and was determined to explore each of the places,
to see if they lived up to the exotic images that their names
had conjured in me. Sometimes all we found at these places
was a hillside or a cluster of farmhouses, or an abandoned
church or curling rink, but always I thought they were worth
the journey. Even when the reality behind the name
was somewhat mundane, it was satisfying to find something undiscovered so close to home. I began to see that
the closer I looked, the more I could find in each of
these places.

"Most beautiful country in the world," Dad often said on our rambles, and there was never any doubt in our minds that it was true.

As we wandered the countryside, each place we passed was connected to the others through webs of stories. Dad told us who lived at each farmhouse, who had owned it before, who was married to whom. He seemed to know everyone and their particular place, and he loved to stop in and visit people off the beaten path. Many times we wandered in unfamiliar farmyards while Dad and Mom talked to the farmers and ranchers. We got to know every farm dog in the district.

But even more than the factor of ownership, a place was marked in Dad's stories by the disasters that had occurred there. We passed the farm where the man had got his shirt-sleeve caught in a baler and the machine had pulled him in; the place where the teenager had been run over by a tractor (driven by his twelve-year-old brother); the farm where a man's .22 rifle had accidentally gone off in his combine and shot him in the temple. In the last case Dad had embellished the story with an account of the combine driving on with the dying man slumped over the wheel. When it reached the end of the field it roared into a stand of poplar saplings, dragging them into the intake.

There were numerous stories of farmers dying pinned under their tractors. In some shops and barns that we visited, there were lurid Co-op calendars from the fifties that enumerated the previous year's farm accidents and depicted a tractor about to roll over sideways on a hill. The startled farmer was already halfway out of his seat, his hands flung out to the sides, his eyes focused on the rapidly approaching ground. You could work out the angles to see that he would be crushed by the rolling machine within a second after he landed.

Dad told us one story of a farmer who had done something like this and had ended up pinned beneath his tractor at the bottom of a ravine. His spine was crushed under the rear wheel, his internal organs hopelessly pulped. But he remained alive—and conscious—for a long time. And at least one of his hands was free. We know this because he managed to find a sharp rock in the unturned earth, and in the last hours or minutes of his life he used that rock to scratch his last will and testament onto the tractor's fender.

To me this was almost unbelievable, even for one of Dad's stories. I knew that in such a situation I would never think of such a thing, and I felt an awestruck admiration for the stoicism of this nameless martyr farmer, who came to symbolize the situation of all farmers in general—existing in a state of hideous adversity, yet somehow scratching out a bit of dignity from the situation. I tried to imagine writing *East quarter goes to Butch. Emma gets pasture + horses. Rest to Char. Signed John.* I would never, ever, have written that, if I could have written anything at all in such a state. I would have been more likely to attempt some memorable last words. *God damn Massey Ferguson* or some such thing.

In those years, farms seemed to me more like war zones than agricultural operations. Our own cousin Marty had climbed inside a combine at the age of twelve and had impaled his forearm on a six-inch blade. He had a colossal purple scar to show for his attempt to explore the inner secrets of agriculture. Uncle Eddy, who was the only real farmer left in the family, was also a testament to the dangers of farm life. He had several fingers and half a thumb missing, from various accidents over the years: grain augurs, power takeoffs, pulleys, belts, chains. I came to regard the names of farm implements—Case, IH, Massey, C.I.L., John Deere— as if they were the names of bombs or enemy tanks. They were louring, gnashing satanic mills, ravenous for human flesh. In my imagination, the Grim Reaper didn't carry a scythe; he drove a combine.

I suppose Dad's stories of farm carnage were intended to scare us into being careful around our own farm, but I never thought of our farm as a danger zone because the machinery was usually owned and operated by others. Art and Jean Waddington rented our land and grew the crops on it, so they always ran the combine and the tractor and the grain augur. We made lunches for them during harvest, and occasionally I drove their grain truck in the field, but I was never close to power takeoffs or rotating blades. I firmly believed that *other* farms were dangerous, but I knew our own farm couldn't possibly be.

Even so, there was at least one moment when I came close to being a character in the ubiquitous legendry of agricultural disaster. We were loading hay bales into the loft of the barn, and we had borrowed a conveyor machine to lift them up there. It had a small engine attached to a long chain studded with spikes that grabbed each bale and slid it up the railing. Glenn and I waited in the loft for the bales to come up, and then we stacked them. But sometimes there were no bales on the conveyor and we had to stand there while Mom and Dad brought them off the wagon. I remember standing in the doorway of the loft, looking down at that chain full of spikes that travelled up the railing and then turned sharply at the end and moved back down. I liked the way they turned so suddenly. And I put my foot up toward the edge of the chain, just to see what would happen.

I guess I thought the spikes would thump harmlessly against the toe of my rubber boot. But a pair of them instantly impaled the boot and yanked it right off my foot. It caught in the space between the chain and the rail, quivering and flopping there like an injured animal. Then suddenly the machine spat the boot out and it thumped on the floor beside me.

I looked down at my foot, which I was still holding up in the air. The front of my sock was shredded. The spikes had passed neatly between my toes without touching me.

"That," Glenn said, pointing at the ribboned boot, "could've been your leg."

I had to bribe him to prevent him from telling Mom and Dad.

Guns were a big part of farm life too, and hunting was one of our most common reasons for rambling. Every able-bodied rural male in the north was by definition a hunter. Very few of these men actually needed the meat for subsistence, but still there was a sense of atavistic pride involved in providing meals for one's family. There was also a general belief that it was good for you to live off the land, that eating wild game was not only tastier but also healthier and somehow more honest than eating grocery store meat. Furthermore, hunting was thought of as a kind of rural philanthropy, since the hunters promised to control the populations of animals— ducks, geese, deer—that threatened to feed on farmers' crops. It was basically a moral imperative to hunt as often and as diligently as you could.

But that wasn't the reason people did it, of course. They did it for the excitement, the camaraderie, the thrill of the ambush, the chase. They also did it because it was simply what they had grown up doing. For farm boys, hunting had always been even more compulsory than hockey. The question was not whether you would hunt but what size of gun you would be allowed to shoot. The most favoured boys were firing twelve-gauge shotguns by the time they reached grade six. Glenn and I started out wandering the back forty with pellet guns and slingshots, taking aim at birds and squirrels and just about anything else that moved. Later I was given a little .410 shotgun, which I passed down to Glenn when I got a twenty-gauge for my fifteenth birthday.

When we hunted with Dad, it always involved driving. He never hunted near the farm, partly for safety reasons and partly because he had a paradoxical desire to encourage game birds to live there. One fall when ducks were eating our barley crop, he preferred to drive out to the field three times a day to scare them off rather than lying in wait to blast them out of the sky. Whenever partridges or prairie chickens showed up in our yard, he would reach not for his shotgun but for his camera. He counted it as a blessing to be visited by them, and he often expressed his hopes that they would establish a family in the bush behind the house. Those few times in the spring when we heard the frantic drumming of the male grouse, he was delirious with expectation.

"Bet we'll have baby ones this year," he would say.

But in the fall, anywhere more than five miles from our house, these same birds were seen as the quarry. When we hunted for partridge and prairie chicken we wandered every back road within several municipalities, watching for the suddenly dumb birds along the roadside or at the edges of fields. Dad had a theory that the partridges got stupid in the fall because they ate the seeds of rosehips. He claimed those seeds were hallucinogenic, though he never told us how he knew. I sometimes wondered if he had tested them himself, trying to get inside the inscrutable mind of the grouse.

I spent many mornings and late afternoons on the road with Dad, scoping out duck and goose hunting spots, always on the lookout for a rosehip-stoned partridge. Despite all the practice, I was far from successful when the time came to pull the trigger. In all my years of hunting, in hundreds of shots fired up at the innocent sky, I never once hit a duck or a goose. I wish I could say I wasn't trying to hit them, but I was. I just couldn't get the trick of leading them correctly, and I guess I was a flock shooter—which in Dad's vocabulary was a term of the utmost contempt. No one ever ridiculed me for my lack of accuracy, though; not even Glenn, who brought down several birds with his pea-shooter shotgun. There was a silent sympathy for me on each of our hunting trips. I was brought along as something of a charity case.

I loved hunting anyway, not so much for the shooting as for the chance to be outside, wandering in new places. We hid in cattails, we waded at the edges of swamps. I ran to retrieve downed birds, since we could never trust our dogs to perform such a task. When hunting, I got to be out in the most glorious of Saskatchewan seasons, mosquitoless and mud-luscious and all the more precious for the imminence of winter. Hunting was usually a contemplative time for me, despite the presence of weapons. We walked along cutlines, huddled in straw-lined goose pits, hunkered at the edges of sloughs. Or else we just drove, slowly, with the windows down and the smoky air of fall pouring over us. We talked about where we'd seen birds other years, where we should try this evening, how much time was left until the magical moment of half an hour after sunset, when all hunting had to stop.

Mom often came along when we were hunting for partridges, though she didn't have her own gun. She was just there to enjoy the ride, to watch the countryside change in the fading light. She loved to eat partridge, as we all did, but she was less fond of duck and she refused to cook geese at all, apparently because of some spectacular failures at goose cooking in a time before I can remember. Partridge hunting was the family hunt. Sometimes we would all go along on what was really an excuse for another drive, a ramble, a kind of Everyman's progress over the territory that Mom and Dad knew so well.

Later in the season my role was to push bush. The quarry was white-tailed deer, and the modus operandi of pushing bush was that one hunter would walk slowly through a stand of forest while another waited in a cutline or along the edge of the bush for a deer to be flushed out. I had been given Uncle Hank's old rifle, a lever-action Winchester 30-30 that looked exactly like the kind I'd seen in Hollywood westerns. These guns had changed little since the end of the nineteenth century. But Uncle Hank had shot deer and elk with it, and it was still a powerful gun. If I encountered a deer at relatively close range, and if I could hold the gun steady, and if I could get my half-frozen trigger finger to work, I could probably have killed a deer. But they were as safe as ducks and geese in my vicinity. I shot at them only twice, at great distances, with Dad beside me coaching. It was clear to me quite early on in my deer-hunting career that my most productive role would be that of bush pusher, slowly herding deer toward Dad and the other hunters.

I will admit that I never liked the geometry of bush pushing, the fact that I would be walking eventually into the line of fire. All the blaze-orange clothing I could festoon myself with was not enough to make me feel particularly safe. But what I worried about more than the bullets was getting lost. I had been in the bush many times, up at our cabin and near Uncle Eddy's farm and at Leonard's Ranch, but in those places I always knew the areas well, knew where the roads and fencelines and power lines went. If I got lost, eventually I would find something I recognized. But when we were hunting I was usually in places I had never been before. Even if I did find a fence or a cutline, it didn't mean I would know which way to turn.

Dad had given me all the safety tips, showing me how to keep from walking in circles by picking a far-off tree trunk to aim for while you stepped around others and through brambles, sidestepping puddles and ponds. "Don't take your eyes off that tree," he said. "And when you get to it, pick another one off in the distance and head for it. That way you'll eventually find a field, or a road. The way people get lost is by going in circles." The prospect of going in circles was terrifying, but I never said anything to Dad about it. I took solace in the knowledge that there was a last resort: the universal hunter's SOS signal of three quick gunshots, which means "Help!"

I got lost only once. It was in November, and there was half a foot of snow on the ground; fresh snow, the best conditions for tracking deer. We had driven a long way back in the bush, somewhere to the west of town. It was near Bluebell, I think, but other than that I didn't have much of a clue where we were. Dad's friends Ron and Greg were in another truck, ready for anything, as always. We saw many lines of deer tracks trailing through the snow at the edge of a field, most of them cutting into a large stand of poplars and scrub willows that appeared to continue along the edge of the field for at least a mile. We had a conference with Ron and Greg, and the decision was made that I would start at this end and push the bush straight to the west, which would take me through a cutline and finally to another field, where Dad and Ron would be waiting. Greg would push the bush from farther north toward the same field.

I started in, following a few sets of the tracks, wondering how long ago the deer had passed. The snow was deeper in the bush, as it often is, and in places banks of tall grass sloughed off their snow as I stepped through. The trees were not as close together as they had looked, and there was more underbrush: clumps of rose bushes with shrivelled raisin-like rosehips showing bright red against the monochromatic background, poplar saplings and flexible red willows with branches that whipped against my jacket as I passed. I held the gun barrel pointed slightly downward to keep snow from sliding down the barrel.

It was cold, and I was wearing woollen gloves, which was a mistake. The gun was slippery in them, and ungainly. I would have to pull them off and drop them in the snow before I could fire. It would have been much better if I could do without them, as Dad and Ron did, but my hands always got too cold from touching the metal of the gun.

The deer tracks veered off in different directions, but I followed one set, past a lone spruce tree and into a stand of more mature poplars. It was easier walking here. Down in a little hollow I saw two deer beds: shallow, icy depressions in the snow where the deer had slept, their body heat melting the snow into shiny, translucent bowls. There were even a few hairs stuck in the ice, along with pieces of dark brown poplar leaves. They had slept there last night, or maybe even today. Deer are often nocturnal and sleep in the afternoons. They might have been here minutes ago.

I followed the tracks over a little ridge and down the other side, into what looked from a distance like a clearing. But it wasn't. As I got nearer, the trees became shorter and closer together. There were large, thick clumps of willows now, and tall grass weighed down with snow. And a little farther, where the ground seemed to flatten out completely, an expanse of cattails.

A swamp. It wasn't supposed to be there.

For the first time I looked up at the sky. It was like a fluorescent light: an even, cool illumination emanated from the entire firmament, which was swathed in a single layer of cloud. The direction of the sun was anybody's guess. I turned to look behind myself at my shuffling footprints that disappeared over the ridge, and as I did this I pulled off my left glove with my teeth and reached into my jacket pocket where I already knew the compass wouldn't be. I had been fooling around with it at home, trying to settle a bet with Glenn about whether the house was built on a true-north angle or not. It was in my bedroom, on my dresser. Not that I knew how to use it, but it would have functioned as at least a talisman, a symbol of security, of orientation. I watched my own tracks and the tracks of the deer receding at the top of the ridge as if they disappeared over the edge of the earth. This was what lost meant. I had wondered what it would be like. I had thought it would be alarming but instead it was strangely dreamlike. The situation was too serious to get angry at myself, to swear, to throw my gloves in the snow and rage. No. I was going to have to get myself out of this or I would freeze to death out here.

A forest becomes something entirely different when you finally admit to yourself that you have no idea where you are. Looking around, three hundred and sixty degrees, and seeing not a trace of human presence except your own muddled footprints, is bewildering. I no longer belonged here. This was not my home. The dormant trees, the snow, the flat expanse of the swamp, the undifferentiated picture of forest all around me—in all of it I saw only the signs of my displacement, my foreignness.

I had been walking for twenty minutes, maybe thirty. I knew I could follow my tracks and eventually get back to where Dad had dropped me off. But that wouldn't do me any good because both the trucks were long gone; they were waiting on the other side of the bush. It seemed best to go on. But I couldn't risk the swamp because I knew the ice would only be a few inches thick, and in swampy areas it is often highly unstable because the water is warmed or disturbed by swamp gases. I had snowmobiled across swamps even in January and found patches of soft, mushy ice. I would have to go around this one.

The walking was much more difficult now, and I noticed my breathing. Not panting, yet, but working hard, harder than necessary, harder than made sense. I trudged onward, past clumps of cattails and tall stands of wild-rice-like grasses that shook as I brushed against them and dropped litters of light brown seeds on me. There was more deadfall here to step over, to balance on, sometimes to walk along like a tightrope walker, avoiding the branches and brambles on the forest floor. I was sure the other field was on the far side of the swamp. It was no time to second-guess myself, no time to try a different direction. I kept my eyes on a tamarack across the swamp, intending to get there and reset my bearings, to climb the slight hill toward what already looked like another clearing beyond.

I began to hurry. Soon they would be wondering where I was. Maybe they would drive back to the starting place to look for me. I tried to imagine what they would do once they realized I was lost, but their motives, even their good sense, seemed entirely in doubt. I had no idea what they would do. Maybe they *would* turn around and go back to the field where I'd started from.

Then I stumbled on hidden deadfall and the gun slipped from my hands. It made a clean, long, rifle-shaped hole in the snow. I dropped down on my knees and groped for it under the hole, not allowing myself to even think about what would happen if it was gone. For a few seconds I felt nothing but branches, but then finally I sensed the slippery shape of the barrel. I reached under it with my other hand and lifted it out, cradling it like an armload of firewood. I rubbed the snow off the stock, opened the magazine and blew snow out of it, tapped the barrel against a tree to dislodge anything that might be stuck in there.

I knew now that I couldn't fire the gun except as a last resort. I had heard of gun barrels exploding because they were plugged with mud, and I imagined snow might do the same thing.

That meant I had no emergency signal.

I looked at my watch: about forty-five minutes until sunset. I had no food, no water, not even a book of matches. I stayed on my knees for a while, looking out at the pattern of trees on the far side of the swamp. My breath hung around my head like a swarm of insects.

"Dad!" I shouted over the swamp, toward the hill on the far side and the clearing I imagined there. "Dad!"

"What?"

I lurched around. The voice had come from behind me, and it wasn't far away.

"Where are you?" he said.

"Here!" I scrambled to my feet and ran headlong through the branches and brambles and swaying grasses, holding the gun sideways in front of me like a commando. I pushed through a clump of willows and saw a sudden opening in the forest. Dad was standing there in his red suit and orange tuque, sipping from a Thermos cup.

"You didn't get down in the swamp there, did you?" he said when I was close enough to see the concern on his face. "We'd've never found you in there."

"No no. I was just following tracks," I said. "Could've swore I sent a buck right toward you."

This time, I don't think he believed me.

III

⁓

Unearth

A northern still life at Fraser's Museum.

MYSTERIES

The guns, the bombs, the Fiddler boys, and the various rumours of violent crimes had long accustomed me to the idea that Meadow Lake could be a dangerous place, but I only gradually came to realize that Dad was sometimes connected to those dangers. It took me a long time to even comprehend exactly what Dad did for a living. Mom was a nurse, which I instinctively understood, but the definition of "lawyer" I had trouble with. When I was about four years old I asked Mom what Dad did all day at work, and she told me "he helps people." She said it in the same tone of enforced certitude that she had used when she answered the question about where babies come from. I wasn't certain what Dad helped people do, but I gathered that it had an air of secrecy about it, perhaps even shame.

"What kind of people does he help?"

"Oh, people with troubles," she said, and her vagueness made me feel I wasn't supposed to inquire further, though I desperately wanted to know what *kind* of troubles.

I had of course eavesdropped on the ubiquitous lawyer jokes that were recounted to Dad on street corners, in living rooms, at the office. He even told them himself from time to time. On the other hand, in my preschool years I used to watch *Perry Mason* every afternoon with our babysitter Mrs. Toews. I could imagine Dad as a courtroom dynamo like Perry Mason, rooting out corruption through the vigour of his questioning, forcing criminals to break down on the stand and admit their misdeeds. Certainly, that was what it felt like when he interrogated *us* about our own various transgressions. We learned early on that it's difficult to keep a secret from someone who cross-examines for a living.

Did you cut Glenn's hair off and tell him to go throw it in the garbage?

No–ooo.

Did you?

I never.

DID YOU?

Nuh–uh.

Well why're there bits of red hair all over your hands, then?

I— He WANTED me to!

Although Dad often mingled truth and fiction in his own stories, he did make a clear distinction between the "fibbing" in stories and the outright lies that we sometimes tried to get away with. We simultaneously feared and admired his ability to drag the truth out of us with little more than a well-chosen question, a stern glance. It seemed inevitable that he would find out everything we did. Maybe this was why I was so fascinated with what he did at work: I wanted to discover the secret of his omniscience.

In response to much cajoling and questioning on my part, Dad eventually agreed to take me with him one day to court. I was five. I remember being impressed by the wooden benches of the courtroom, which reminded me of church, except there were no planks to kneel on. The room was windowless. I sat near the back, my feet dangling from the edge of the bench. Then we had to stand up and sit down, also like in church. The highlight of the day was to see Dad walking up the centre aisle with two other men, all of them wearing long black gowns. I hardly recognized him. I couldn't wait to get back home and tell Glenn and Michelle: *Dad wears a dress at work!* But aside from the sartorial novelty, the trial quickly became boring. One man stood up, and then Dad, and then another man. They used words like *fiduciary* and *entailment* and *tort.* This was nothing like Perry Mason's trials, where the lawyers wore suits and spoke in English and where the criminals were brought to tears on the witness stand. There weren't even any witnesses this time, as I recall. I gazed listlessly down at my feet, which swung like pendulums, measuring out the afternoon. It was enough to cure me of my curiosity for a long time.

Not long after this, Glenn also went to court with Dad, despite my warnings that he wouldn't like it. He must have had Perry Mason on the brain, too, because in the middle of the proceedings he called out, "Put that man in jail, Daddy!" Unfortunately, the man in question was Dad's client. Our court visits were discontinued after that, and Michelle never got her turn.

By the time we moved out to the farm I was starting to get a clearer idea about Dad's job and his place in the community. He helped some people, as Mom had said, but he also made enemies. At the end of every trial, win or lose, there would always be at least one person who hated him. He accepted this with equanimity most of the time, but it must have been difficult, especially in such a small community where everyone knew him, and where certain grudges were passed down through the generations. He was sometimes the Crown prosecutor on drug-related cases throughout northwestern Saskatchewan, which meant that he attracted the resentment of a whole class of criminals. Other people hated him because he had represented their ex-spouses in divorce trials, or he had initiated lawsuits or criminal proceedings against them or their friends. For any small-town lawyer, that kind of bitterness is almost impossible to avoid.

During my teen years I was only dimly aware of the specific controversies Dad was involved in. I knew he got phone calls at all hours, and that sometimes they weren't pleasant ones. I knew he sometimes received threats too. But he wasn't unpopular; in fact he seemed to be widely respected in town. He was one of only a few people in the district who was known to virtually everyone—Native and non-Native, young and old, farmers and town dwellers. He made a real effort to get acquainted with everyone in the surrounding area, and the people who met him remembered him. It was easy to focus on this positive side of things, and to forget about Dad's enemies.

One of the first times I recognized the frightening aspects of Dad's job was when I was fourteen and he showed us the evidence photos from a murder trial he was working on. I don't even recall if he was the prosecutor or the defence counsel, and I don't think I ever heard the outcome of the trial. But those photos have stayed with me. It was a stabbing.

The body was lying face down on a blood-soaked bed. There was blood on the walls, the ceiling, the light fixture above the bed, and all over the victim's clothes: a white T-shirt and jeans that were now almost the same wet burgundy colour as the bed. I couldn't believe the quantity of blood. It was as though it had come welling up out of the mattress, like something in *The Shining* or *The Amityville Horror.* Except it had none of the aestheticized glamour of movies and books. The corpse was not beautiful, the lighting was harsh and unsubtle, and the preponderance of red in the picture had caused a kind of blue-shift in the photo process, tinting the unbloodied parts of the walls an icy aquamarine. It was so difficult to comprehend that this was *real,* and that my father had to deal with the reality of it. I tried to imagine him formulating a case, going over the details of a slaughter like this, digging for more information. It was hard to believe this was the same person who puttered around in the garden every evening, who told outlandish and wonderful stories about the north. He was regularly exposed to the most violent and depraved aspects of our community and yet he still clearly loved the place. Not everyone would have been able to do so.

It was even dangerous for him sometimes. Once when he was crossing Main Street, a half-ton truck accelerated through the intersection and he had to jump aside to avoid being hit. The driver, whom I'll call Mrs. Dempsey, had been glaring directly at him as the truck sped toward him, and she looked back over her shoulder when she'd gone by. Dad had represented a client in a lawsuit against Mrs. Dempsey many years earlier. This was not the first threat he received from her, and I don't think it was the last.

We never knew where the next threat would come from. Once when Mom and Dad were hunting south of town, they drove across some ranchland belonging to a farmer who had some reason or other to hate Dad. They discovered this only when the farmer's half-ton ground to a halt beside them and Dad was confronted with the barrel of a rifle pointing in his face.

"You're trespassing, Ray."

He was able to talk his way out of the situation, but we never did learn how he managed it. Dad always downplayed these incidents, unlike most of the stories he told about his experiences in the north. In fact he and Mom didn't even mention this one until about a year after it had happened, by which time it struck Dad as almost comical, like the old cartoons of Hatfields and McCoys. Hillbilly territorialism seemed harmless enough from a distance.

"A lotta crazies in this world," Dad said, chuckling. But I saw that Mom wasn't laughing at all.

Another time, when Dad was representing an RCMP officer's wife in a divorce settlement, our farm became the site of a one-man stakeout operation. The cop waited on the highway and stopped Dad almost every time he drove past. He would check over every inch of the car, looking for potential violations, even when he had inspected it the previous day. He made no secret about what he was doing. We wondered what would happen if we ever *needed* the police and this guy showed up.

I imagine there were other threats, near-misses, and intimidations that I never found out about. Mom and Dad didn't want us to worry. But we did learn about one of them because it became infamous. It involved a man I'll call Vern Michulak, who had been one of the town's most prominent and successful businessmen. At times it seemed that he owned half the town, though I suppose the most he really owned was about a fifth of the retail businesses. Everyone shopped in his stores, and most people in town had stopped in at his Ford dealership to look at the selection of cars and trucks. Vern was also well known for his extensive gun collection, which ranged from old black-powder shotguns to high-powered modern rifles.

In March of 1986, an RCMP investigation led to charges of fraud at Michulak's Ford dealership. The Crown alleged that the mileage had been readjusted on some of the used cars, and the tax records were incomplete. Dad was one of the lawyers on hand when police stormed the dealership and seized the documents, and I think he had something to do with the prosecution of the case. Michulak was eventually found guilty and was levied several fines. After that, his businesses began to falter and his personal life fell into disarray. A family member later told the police that on or about August 19, 1988, Michulak stopped taking the lithium chloride medication that controlled his mood swings.

On that same day, Michulak phoned the RCMP and left a message saying that he had information about an international spy ring and that he needed to speak to several officers immediately. The police felt the call was either a joke or was crazy, so they didn't respond. A witness later said Michulak firmly believed that satellites were spying on him and that someone was trying to kill him. He kept a loaded rifle in his truck for protection.

Around midnight on August 26, an unidentified person rammed a vehicle into an unoccupied Dodge van parked on a roadside east of Meadow Lake, and then fired a rifle at the van's rear passenger compartment. Police later recovered a 130-grain Spitzer boat-tail bullet from a hole in the van's refrigerator.

The next day, someone phoned the RCMP to report that Vern Michulak was driving through town firing a hunting rifle out the window of his truck. Everyone knew he was accustomed to shooting from this position. Because of a childhood illness and a serious accident later in life, Michulak's mobility was severely restricted, and he had received special dispensation from the wildlife authorities to hunt from his vehicle. He was known to be an expert marksman.

Father Maurice, the pastor of our church, later told my dad that Vern Michulak appeared at the rectory that same Saturday afternoon and asked if Ray Cariou would be there for mass the next morning. "I don't know," Father Maurice replied. And he must have noticed something strange about this man, because when Michulak asked him if he knew where Ray Cariou lived, the priest lied, said he didn't know.

That was the end of the conversation. A witness later reported that as Michulak was driving away from the rectory, he fired a shot at the church itself. According to town legend, the bullet ricocheted off the church bell and left a splash of lead on the brass. This seems unlikely, since the bell is nestled inside the church steeple, seventy feet off the ground, and only a few square inches of metal are visible from the parking lot. But such a shot was not beyond the realm of his marksmanship.

The police didn't catch up with Vern Michulak until ten o'clock the following morning, when a farmhand named

James Moore was found dead in a ditch east of town. He had been shot while fleeing from his vehicle. Michulak had rammed Moore's El Camino for no apparent reason, and then when Moore returned to the scene with a friend, Michulak started shooting at them. When the police arrived, Michulak was still sitting in his truck less than two hundred yards from the body, mumbling about satellites and pictures from the sky and international conspiracies. Just before Michulak handed over the homicide weapon, the negotiator said to him, "You've killed somebody." Michulak's only response was, "Good."

Mom and Dad didn't talk about Vern Michulak much after the murder, though they corroborated some of the stories I had heard from other sources, and they told me what the priest had said: that Michulak had asked about Dad at the church only a few hours before he drove out of town to kill someone else.

"Nothing you can do when a kook like that comes along," Dad said. But I knew the murder had affected him and Mom deeply, because they did do something. One evening, not long after Father Maurice told him what had happened at church, Dad walked out to the end of our driveway and removed the wooden sign that read "Ray and Melba Cariou and Family."

The empty signpost stood there at the edge of the road for a decade.

Long after the murder, Mom and Dad told me about something that had happened a few years before it—the year of my high-school graduation, the summer I left Meadow Lake for university. An envelope had arrived at Dad's office containing a single sheet of paper. It was a photocopy of my graduation picture, which had been published in the local newspaper that spring along with photos of all my other classmates. My picture had been magnified several times until it nearly filled the page, and there were four bullet holes in my face.

Dad took it immediately to the RCMP, who dusted it for fingerprints, but nothing was found. Whoever had done this had been careful. The most the police could do was to speculate, from the size of the holes, that the bullets had been fired from a hunting rifle. They may have had suspects, but without more evidence, all they could do was wait—wait for something else to happen.

Mom and Dad felt they shouldn't tell me at the time, and I suppose this was for the best. I'm not sure what I would have thought if they had told me then. I had gotten over my childhood fearfulness by that time, and had even adopted some teenage recklessness, but learning about that picture would still have been bewildering, as it is to me even now. It's bizarre to remember myself as I was that summer—dreamy, ardently in love with my high-school girlfriend, full of confidence and anxiety about my coming life in the city—and to realize that at the same time, someone was tacking my image to a tree or a fence post, stepping back a good distance, raising a rifle, and firing.

It makes me wonder: what else do I not know about myself?

Bull riders start young in Meadow Lake.
(MARLOW ESAU PHOTO)

STAMPEDE

I think I was always *going* to leave Meadow Lake, at least from the age of six or seven when I discovered that it was not, after all, the centre of the universe. Anyone who wanted to attend university would necessarily have to make the trip beyond the bounds of the Height of Land, and I had watched generations of high-school graduates do just that. Few of them returned. It was a foregone conclusion that I would follow their venerable tradition of leaving, so in my last years of high school it sometimes seemed like I had already left.

On the other hand, when I did go, I didn't feel like I was leaving. I would be back at Thanksgiving, at Christmas, and several times during the term. I would look for a summer job in Meadow Lake. I was living away from home, but it was only temporary, only tentative. My bedroom at the farm remained my bedroom, complete with motocross posters, curling trophies, 4-H ribbons, stamp collection, car magazines, *Star Wars* collectibles, Def Leppard banner, and all the other assorted paraphernalia of Meadow Lake teenagehood. At my insistence, Mom left the room like that for a decade or so.

It's difficult to mark a time or place or event at which I crossed from Meadow Lake to the outside world. There was no moment when I chose exile, no last look back, no great boat journey to separate me finally from the place. There were no real goodbyes; only see-you-laters. I don't remember ever surveying the countryside with a sense of loss, of regret. I would always be back soon, and the place would be the same. There was none of the poignancy and drama of a clear break. I simply began to exist in two places: one a *real* home, and the other temporary, contingent, moveable. I have lived like that ever since.

There was however one moment when I was getting ready to move to Saskatoon for the first time. After loading the last of my cardboard boxes, garbage bags, plastic bins, and suitcases into the back of Uncle Vic's truck, I looked back and saw Mom standing in front of the house, beside the blue spruce tree, crying. She was trying to smile at the same time, and holding her head at a slight angle as if to suggest the incongruity of her conflicting emotions. At first I had no idea what had happened. And then I realized that she thought I was leaving. And for a moment, the shock of it hit me too: I *was* leaving, abandoning my home, going forth into the dangerous world. But it didn't feel true.

"It's okay, Mom," I said. "I'll be back in a few weeks."

Even now, seventeen years later, that is still how I say goodbye.

After a succession of moves to Saskatoon each fall and back home for the summer, I graduated from university and began going wider afield, first to Regina, then Toronto, then back to

Saskatoon, and back to Toronto. I was following opportunities in these cities, and I enjoyed living in them all, but I never held any illusions that they were home. At the same time, my feeling of distance from Meadow Lake gradually increased. Between visits, I spoke to Mom and Dad regularly on the phone, but these conversations didn't tell me much about the place. By then most of my friends had moved away from Meadow Lake, so my only real contact with the area was through my parents. Mostly when I talked to them, they were interested in weather.

"What's it like there?" Mom would ask, and I would dutifully give my report, before she began her disquisition on the temperature, moisture, and wind readings in Meadow Lake since the last time we had spoken. Always it was bad news for the farmers.

"I sure hope it smartens up soon," she would say, "or the farmers'll be in trouble. Well, I don't want to keep you long, so here's Dad."

"Hi, Dad."

"Hi. So what's the weather like there?"

The miracle of telecommunications just didn't work for Dad. Whereas in person he would give you a long and marvellous story in response to the simplest question, on the phone he was the opposite: gruff, monosyllabic, inscrutable. He was so uncomfortable with the technology that he often hung up without saying goodbye.

"Yep, okay." Click.

"Bye, Dad."

At the end of a conversation, I would know everything about the weather in Meadow Lake, but virtually nothing else.

Partly this fixation on weather was related to their agricultural and horticultural pursuits. To gardeners and farmers, the atmospheric conditions can take on extraordinary proportions. Mom had come by this honestly. Her dad, Grandpa Strelau, had been a farmer, and he was obsessed with weather too. After he died, we were going through his papers and someone discovered a five-year diary that consisted entirely of daily temperature and precipitation records, occasionally followed by a one-word commentary such as "cloudy" or "frost." If anyone should ever want to study the meteorology of Canwood, Saskatchewan, this diary will be an invaluable resource.

For Mom and Dad, I think the conversations about weather were also very much about distance. They were fascinated with the idea that I could be suffering through a heat wave in Toronto or wherever I was, while in Meadow Lake there was still frost at night. It was a matter of marvel, of wonder, and I think it reinforced in them the idea that I was living in a different world altogether.

I suppose I wasn't immune to such thinking either. After all, at a certain level I still felt I belonged in a place that I was thousands of miles away from—a place where it was unlikely I would ever live again. The fact that I lived in a double space, an unreal space, became most visible to me whenever I did go home. The changes there were disconcerting. New buildings, new businesses, new people. Sometimes these were welcome, but most of the time they were disturbances, interruptions in the clean orderliness of my memory. Things were not supposed to change there. Perhaps complete exile from Meadow Lake would have been more comfortable than these repeated returns to a place that was no longer exactly what I remembered.

Not only did I start to feel like I was losing touch with Meadow Lake but I also realized that it was losing touch with me. This became most noticeable to me one year when I went to the Meadow Lake Stampede. I was living in Regina by that time, working my first real job, writing speeches for the provincial health department. I had been away from home for six or seven years and didn't live there in the summers anymore, though I returned for several weeks each year. I was a little bit smug then, a little too proud of myself for having made my way past the Height of Land, having "escaped," as some of my fellow escapees liked to say. I had started to think of Meadow Lake as a quaint but backward place—"a good place to come *from*," I told my city friends.

I decided to revisit the stampede that year out of a vague anthropological interest, I suppose. I wanted to see with my new worldly eyes this event that was so crucial to Meadow Lake's definition of itself. The stampede goes right back to the beginning of Meadow Lake's history as a homestead settlement, and over the years it has contributed a great deal to the wild-west mythology of the region. Meadow Lake's hockey team is called the Stampeders, and the town's only mascot is the bronc-rider statue on the boulevard, the one we used to pelt with snowballs when I was a kid. The early cowboys and organizers of the stampede—Jimmy Evans, Slim Knox, Alf Bronken, Dooley Walker—are probably better known than the founders of the town. The first stampede grew out of an informal community picnic held in the summer of 1920, perhaps organized with the intention of keeping people's minds off the catastrophe of the Great Fire the previous summer. George Stewart, the farmer who had stood on the sod roof of his barn dousing flames a year earlier, was now the host of this first rodeo. Only a few miles away, the vast expanses of charred forest began. Yet these pioneers were there to celebrate survival, and to tell their stories of hardship, and to demonstrate the skills and strength that gave them hope for their futures in this place.

Meadow Lakers have long felt an uncharacteristic but well-justified civic pride in their stampede. For years it was billed as the country's second-largest pro rodeo, next only to Calgary's extravaganza. The Meadow Lake Stampede was always held the weekend before Calgary's, and was thought to be a suitable lead-up to that most famous festival of western identity. But the Meadow Lake Stampede fell upon hard times in recent years, and now it has been cancelled altogether because of financial and logistical problems. The proximity to Calgary's rodeo became a liability as more and more of the pros opted to skip Meadow Lake in order to prepare for Calgary. Purse money dropped, attendance dropped, and eventually the stampede was replaced by a much smaller amateur "Bullarama" held in the hockey rink.

In my era, most locals (at least the adults) didn't actually spend much time at the stampede, except to watch the chuckwagon races in the evenings. Before the stampede became professionalized, when a lot of local men and women competed, I think it was different. But in recent years there have been only a few Meadow Lake cowboys and cowgirls on the professional circuit, so the stampede came to have the feel of an event that wasn't quite local. It was more like a big, sprawling road show that rolled into town for four or five days, complete with a midway and a Saturday-night dance that was virtually guaranteed to end in a brawl. So while the people of Meadow Lake felt a fierce ownership over the stampede, in a sense it was no longer theirs. The stampede became a place that was noplace, an event that carried itself around the countryside all summer. The carnies in the midway, the cowboys, the announcers, the rodeo clowns—all of them were the perfect models of the nomad, wandering their itinerant circuit, repeating their performances again and again in one place after another. The carnies especially seemed to be the most unrooted of people, at home nowhere but in their trailers and their booths, the latter festooned with the stuffed toys and cotton candy and plastic trinkets that small-town kids' fantasies are made of.

I did love the stampede when I was a kid, more for the midway than the rodeo. I rode the Tilt-a-Whirl and the Scrambler and the chuffing, pendulum-like Rock-a-Sky until I was completely addled with mechanical motion. The point was to bring myself to physical illness so I could brag about it later. The pathway to glorified vomiting was assured if I managed to scam a free tin of snuff from the Copenhagen Chewing Tobacco booth and cram a fingerful into my bottom lip.

But I also treasured the less sensationalistic aspects of the stampede, like the piney smell of the wood chips that covered the ground between the booths, a smell that almost disguised the repellent odours wafting from the corndog stands near the rodeo entrance. And I had always been addicted to the dime toss, because it was the only game I was any good at. I had learned to lick my palm and get the dime good and wet before tossing it in a high arc over the assembled mountain of dishware. With a liberal application of saliva, I could make a flying dime stop on a—well, on a saucer, if not on a dime. My trick was responsible for more than a few birthday and Christmas and Mother's Day presents over the years. Most of the other games also involved some kind of tossing—ring toss, furry cat toss (the stuffed cats were not tossed but arranged as targets), milk bottle toss (same principle as the cats), darts-and-balloons—but I was hopeless at these contests, despite many dollars' worth of practice.

There was a definite sense of danger about the stampede for me too, since the stampede grounds were the territory of the Fiddler boys and their threatening friends. During stampede, they were there in full force, moving in tight groups like military units, diminutive guerrillas. Many of them hung out under the grandstands, smoking and laughing and sometimes peering through cracks to watch the rodeo on the other side. To me, there was something menacing about the underside of those towering wooden grandstands, with their unpainted posts and their multiplicitous weavings of slats and joists. The whole thing seemed spindly and unstable and rotten when you looked at it from the back, though it was perfectly presentable from the front. From behind, it looked like the kind of place in movies and cop shows where a final shootout would occur (I could see a criminal tumbling from the upper railing, his gun still clutched in his hand), or where a body might be buried. I always refused to go under the grandstands even when it was raining, as it always seemed to be during stampede. Instead I stood out in the open on the wood chips with my cotton candy melting away in the rain, holding out my palm to get my dimes good and wet, trying not to respond to the taunting of the Milk Bottle carny who was offering me an extra throw for a dollar.

Returning to the stampede after eight or nine years was reassuring in some ways. Much of it was exactly the same. The pony rides were there near the entrance to the parking lot— the ponies tramping their endless sad circles, harnessed to a wheel of metal spokes—and the piddly Ferris wheel that I had scoffed at even as a kid, and most of my favourite rides were still there, except for the Scrambler, which, according to rumour, had gone out of alignment a few years back in some other town and had smashed some poor kid's teeth out. The smells of pine chips and cotton candy and cow shit were there as always. The Copenhagen kiosk now had a neighbouring booth that advertised free sample packets of Bullseye Hickory Smoke Special Barbecue Sauce. The dime toss was gone, the value of dimes having fallen since my childhood and that of cheap crockery having gone up. But most of the other games were there, manned by carnies who may well have been the same ones I had seen as a kid: greasy, nonchalant, drinking endless cups of fountain Coke as they badgered the slow-moving parade of easy marks. The only thing different about them was the increased number of tattoos and body piercings, and the sad lack of snappy messages on their

T-shirts. I had always admired the iron-on transfers on the carny-shirts of the past: *A Touch of Class; I'm with Stupid; Injection Is Nice But I'd Rather Be Blown; Gas, Grass, or Ass— Nobody Rides for Free.* Now they all wore plaid.

There was a storm coming, and the lights of the Ferris wheel and the Rock-a-Sky were luridly festive in the face of the looming clouds. It had already rained daily for the previous week. Just like old times. With the smells, and the menace of the clouds, and the milling multitudes wandering past the booths and through the gates into the rodeo grounds, it was almost enough to awaken a twinge of nostalgia.

After an hour at the midway, during which I earned nothing but tendinitis in my throwing arm and several galling smirks from the throwing-game carnies, I paid my way into the grandstand area in time for the bull riding. Chuckwagons had long been the popular favourites at stampede, but as spectator sports go, sheer insanity always wins over competitive spirit for me. Bull riding is probably the closest thing we have to throwing Christians to the lions. Men are paralyzed, pierced, mutilated, and crushed every year on the circuit, and deaths are not rare. For this—and for the mud—I and my fellow Meadow Lakers had paid our money. Besides, the prospect of men riding huge, frothing, needle-horned behemoths around a shit-filled arena was more than a little reminiscent of my own 4-H days, so I felt a certain distant affinity for the sport.

The action had already begun when I arrived, so I stood at the chain-link fence for a while to watch from close up. The first thing I noticed was that the mud was worse than ever. True chocolate soup gumbo. It was abomasum-deep on the bulls, and when (not if) the riders were flung off, they stuck instantly in place, flat on their backs or head-first or—if they were lucky enough to land right side up—skewered into the gumbo up to their knees. Several of them had to swim their way to the surface before scrambling away from the charging bulls. Still, the riders insisted on wearing their spotless white cowboy hats, which usually flew off within the first three seconds. The rodeo clowns wore a motley of muck on their scarlet costumes. Sometimes they pitched handfuls of mud at the bulls to divert their attention from the earth-bound cowboys.

The bulls themselves were not much impeded by the conditions. They whirled and seesawed and kicked, stirring the mud like cloven-hoofed Mixmasters. A little crowd gathered near me at the edge of the fence where the view of the carnage was best. "C'mon!" they called out. "Get 'im." I didn't know if they were cheering for rider or beast. I didn't know if *I* was either. The bulls had a ferocious dignity despite the streams of slaver and shit that spewed out of them in mid-gyration. Their eyes were dilated with rage, their nostrils blasting vitriol. Even if one of these cowboys should cling to a bull for the required eight seconds, it was clear that the final victor would always be the animal.

I locked my fingers in the chain-link fence as the crowd began to press in. I smelled hot-dog breath and manky hair and sweat, even over the omnipresent odours of mud and dung and fear.

The first nine riders ended up in the mud before their eight seconds were up. The announcer's high-pitched, country-gospel-hour preacher's voice surged in staccato bursts through the ancient loudspeakers mounted on telephone poles beside the track. "There he is, he's out, and around, and—hang in there, lad—and—looks like—OH! He's down, and just before the horn."

The loudest hollers and shrieks were reserved for the clowns, who popped into their rubberized barrels at the last possible instant before the bulls plowed into them. They took wildly unnecessary chances, tapping the bulls on the hindquarters, waving their mud-soaked handkerchiefs in the animals' faces, and scrambling or cartwheeling away just in time. This is what clowns are supposed to be: dangerous, agile, death-defying. Circus clowns are nothing in comparison.

I pushed my way out of the crowd as the second half of the riding was about to begin. I had been lost in the event until this point, unaware of my own place in the crowd, unaware of the identities of the people around me. But now, as I looked up into the grandstands for a likely place to sit for the next part of the show, I felt suddenly conspicuous. No one was looking at me, but that was precisely what made me feel strange. There were more than a thousand faces in the grandstands, and not one of them seemed to recognize me. Some of these people were vaguely familiar to me—perhaps family resemblances or old acquaintances—but I could tell that my dim sense of recognition was not reciprocated. To them I wasn't the Cariou boy, or the one who went off to Regina, or the one who used to go with so-and-so. I was a stranger.

This didn't stop me from climbing up the grandstands and taking a seat there to watch the rest of the event. But it nagged at me. I was no longer one of them; I was an outsider, a city boy I was dressed wrong (no Wranglers, no boots, no ball cap). I had become a tourist in my hometown. Tourists were rare in Meadow Lake, except at stampede, but we always recognized them whenever we saw them. And we always scorned them too, if only because we suspected that they must feel the same about us.

As I watched the cowboys bounce and wheel and flail their arms on the backs of the bulls, I came to think that I was more like the stampede people than the local people. I just passed through town on the way to somewhere else.

On my way out of the rodeo grounds, as I walked between the Copenhagen booth and the wooden pillars of the grandstands, a gang of boys was laughing and whispering. Possibly at me, I thought. They looked to be mostly Native, and they were skinny but tough looking, like the Fiddler boys used to be. As I passed within a few feet of them, they burst suddenly into laughter. *Oh ho ho! Ooowee!* They were certainly looking at me, but I didn't look back. I kept walking, shaking my head slightly and smiling even though I didn't feel like smiling. It was the pose of idiotic goodwill that had got me through some frightening confrontations as a child. I felt no real threat from these boys, but it was clear they were up to no good, and the sound of their laughter brought me back to a time when I would have been nearly paralyzed in such a situation.

"He's a fag anyway," I heard one of them say as I stepped onto the wood-chip avenue that led to the toss games. I shook my head more visibly, more disapprovingly, and I kept walking, past the darts-and-balloons game. Fag. When I was growing up it had almost nothing to do with sexuality. It was simply the universal term for outsider, for pariah, for weakling. Some things about Meadow Lake had not changed at all.

It wasn't until I had slid into the car that I noticed the smell: a cloying molasses-and-vinegar odour that I didn't recognize at first. I was about to look under my seat to find out what was rotting down there when I saw what was on my pant leg. I clambered back out of the car.

"Little bastards," I said, craning my neck to look behind myself.

Barbecue sauce. The back of my pants, from ass to ankle, was coated with thick splatters of Bullseye Hickory Smoke Special Barbecue Sauce. There was a smudge on the car seat too.

I pulled out a clump of quackgrass from the parking lot and used it to wipe off the sauce. But it was no use. Bits of grass now clung to my pants. I was tarred and feathered. Basted by the new Fiddler boys, ready for the grill.

"I hate this fucking place," I said, but I couldn't help laughing. I pictured those little shits stomping on pouches of Hickory Smoke Special, hooting as jets of it leaped out from under their Nikes—practising their aim for the moment when the perfect target came in range: the tourist, the outsider, the fag. How many other people would they get today? Or would I be the only lucky victim?

"Bastards." I almost had to admire their gleeful, reckless xenophobia. How many other people in town would think the same thing as these boys, but not express it?

I could feel the sauce soaking through onto my leg. My jeans would be wrecked, most likely. But what could I do about it now? I peeled them off, rolled them into a sweet-smelling ball, and drove home in my underwear.

Logs piled at Norsask mill.

BLOCKADE

In the spring of 1992, I was nearing the end of my first year in Toronto, where I had started graduate school at the University of Toronto. The city was nothing like home, but it was also nothing like the undifferentiated urban wasteland I had been led to expect. It had neighbourhoods, some of which felt almost like small but crowded towns. The people were polite and friendly most of the time, even on the subway. I could go to plays and concerts and galleries any day of the week. I had made several friends during my short time there, and I was looking forward to making more. It was a shame that everyone back home hated Toronto so much.

But as I revelled in the offerings of the metropolis, I came to feel more and more isolated from Meadow Lake. I wondered how Mom and Dad pictured my life there, amid the grandeur and the glitter of a place they had never visited. I wrote a few letters back home that must have seemed like dispatches from the Moon.

"Went to a place called the Dance Cave last night, where I injured my neck trying to dance like everyone else."

"Heard Ton Koopman play Bach toccatas on the new pipe organ at Knox United."

"Met some friends at the Bovine Sex Club (not what it sounds like!)."

After a while I learned to give fewer details. I didn't consider that my family might be doing the same.

Meanwhile, in Meadow Lake, things were happening. A group of Native protestors started a blockade on a logging road adjacent to a large clearcut on the way to Canoe Lake. They objected to clearcutting and refused to allow the forestry company, Mistik Management, to have access to a stockpile of logs that had been cut the previous winter. They vowed to stay there in their roadside encampment until the company changed its policies. They even made application to have the community instituted as a village: the Northern Hamlet of Wiggins Bay.

I learned about this before it hit the news, because Dad was in the middle of it. He had been the chairman of Mistik Management and the local sawmill for several years, ever since the provincial government had privatized the companies. He was proud of his association with the sawmill, which was jointly owned by the mill employees and the tribal council of the ten local First Nations. In a town where the racial divide had often kept people apart, the mill was a monument of community cooperation. But the alliance had never been easy, and now it looked like the whole enterprise might collapse.

He first mentioned the protest at the end of a phone call, after several minutes of commentary on the weather.

"So," he said, "looks like we've got a blockade now, up by Canoe Lake. Should hit the news in a couple days."

He said it with resignation, as if a blockade was not much different from a drought or an unseasonable frost. Bad weather. But he didn't yet know how bad it would be. There was tension in his voice as he described a few more details— the names of the protestors, their alliances, their willingness to negotiate. He was not in storytelling mode. Maybe he believed at some level that if he didn't turn it into a story it couldn't take on a life of its own.

The media believed it was a story, though. It hit the news much harder than Dad could have imagined. "Standoff in Northern Saskatchewan," the headlines read. "Blockade May Turn Violent." To someone from Meadow Lake, the negotiations might have seemed like a relatively simple matter, something to be settled between the timber company and the blockaders, but in fact the situation was a recipe for national alarm. Maybe in a different year it might not have generated so much concern, but this was less than two years after the Oka crisis, and the whole country was edgy about Native blockades. The reporters poured into town, think-ing—or perhaps hoping—that Meadow Lake would be the next Oka.

The RCMP were on high alert too, and from early on in the dispute, there were rumours that specially armed tactical forces were standing at the ready somewhere nearby. And while most of the protestors were peaceful, others dropped ominous hints of militancy behind the blockade lines. The protestors were joined by two Mohawk warriors who had been part of the resistance at Oka. The presence of reporters intensified the paranoia on both sides of the blockade, and the more people talked about the possibility of violence, the more likely it came to seem. I think Dad felt the pressure of this rhetoric. He was one of the company's main negotiators, and he was their media spokesman. He found himself at the nexus of all the major conflicts in the town: racial, economic, environmental, legal. What he did and said could have serious consequences.

I wasn't sure what to think of the blockade myself. Like many of my urban contemporaries, I sympathized with the environmental statement the protestors were making and with the situation of Saskatchewan's aboriginal people. But on the other hand, I trusted Dad and the people he worked with, and I knew the company had made great strides toward creating a positive atmosphere between non-Natives and Natives in Meadow Lake. From such a distance, all I could do was hope—for mutual understanding, for a diminishment of violent rhetoric, for a peaceful settlement. I had no idea how likely any of that might be.

According to the friends I consulted, in Meadow Lake the reaction to the blockade was mixed. There was some of the racial bias that might have been expected. Some people were offended that "radicals," "shit-disturbers," "welfare bums," and "criminals" were holding the company hostage. Others were disgusted that the blockade was drawing negative publicity to the town. Some people believed the leaders were in it more for themselves than for Mother Earth.

But this was not like Oka, even though the reporters may have wanted it to be. It was not Natives versus whites. The forestry company, after all, was half owned by Native bands. And the blockade caused little inconvenience to the people of Meadow Lake, who could still travel on the Mill Road north to Canoe Lake. The fundamental issue of the protest was not a land claim, as it had been at Oka, but rather a general environmental sensibility, and a specific statement against clearcutting. Many people in Meadow Lake, Native and non-Native, agreed with the protestors' stand on environmental action. One local church raised donations to provide food and other necessities to the protestors. So the town was not as polarized along racial lines as it might have been.

There was, however, a very real concern that the sawmill's stockpile of logs would run out and that the mill would have to be shut down. With layoffs would come the most serious threat of reprisals against the blockaders.

Dad worried about every angle, every possibility.

"They're putting me through my paces, I'll say that," he said in one brief phone call. He was so busy he barely had time for a weather report. "Don't know what good it's doing, but I suppose . . ."

What did he suppose? His voice was pinched, and he exhaled loudly in the receiver. I don't know what he really thought about his role in the crisis, but I suspect he felt the strain of Meadow Lake's contradictions and divisions. He was there to hold them all together, however fitfully, until the time of crisis had passed. That was the best he could hope for.

Mom sent me newspaper clippings as the crisis went on, though I knew she was frustrated by the whole thing and would rather have forgotten about it altogether. "Dad's very tired out by all this," she wrote. It seemed there was nothing any of us could do to help. Certainly from my own position, half a continent away, I was hopelessly out of touch with it all.

I read the clippings as they came, and I compared the stories with the brief accounts I had heard from Mom and Dad. David Suzuki, on tour for his book *The Wisdom of the Elders,* had come to visit the protestors but had been criticized by some locals as an outsider who stepped in without understanding the complexities of the situation. Most of the media began to change their alarmist assumptions after the initial flurry of reports. Once they realized that the standoff was not whites versus Natives but rather that Native people were involved on both sides, they began to back away from the Oka comparison. Some stories mentioned that the protestors were controversial among the Native community too, and that some Native people objected to the militaristic rhetoric of a few of the protestors.

One of these reports contained a perplexing statement that Michelle had already told me about over the telephone. After giving a description of the latest developments in the standoff and quoting Dad on the position of the forestry company, the reporter had added a single sentence about Dad: "Cariou himself has recently reaffirmed his Metis heritage."

This information wasn't entirely a shock to me, but seeing it there in the newspaper was mystifying. Dad had never "reaffirmed his Metis heritage" to us, at least not in so many words. There had been rumours in the family and comments about the dark features of some of the relatives. But Dad himself had red hair and freckles, and so did

Glenn, and so did many of our cousins. The idea of publicly claiming Metis heritage was bizarre.

I wasn't there to see Dad's reaction to the description, though I was told he had laughed about it and had said he'd been misquoted. I never asked him about it. It seemed too strange, too disconnected from my own reality, and for some reason I thought he wouldn't want to talk about it. So I kept my questions secret. I wondered what Dad might have said to the reporter that could have been construed as a statement of Metis identity, and all I could think of was what he had told us the previous Christmas about one of our ancestors. Aunt Anita had been researching our genealogy and had discovered something that linked us with one of Dad's favourite historical figures.

"One of our ancestors was a voyageur," he said. "With Alexander Mackenzie. What do you think of that?"

He showed us a handwritten excerpt from *The Manuscript Journals of Alexander Henry and of David Thompson.* One sentence was marked with a yellow highlighter: "François Beaulieu started with Alexander Mackenzie in 1793 as a voyageur (In 1793 the first successful overland trip to the Pacific was made by Mackenzie)." This François Beaulieu was Dad's direct ancestor, according to the genealogy. And from the wording of the account, it seemed likely that François had accompanied Mackenzie on his historic trek across the continent.

Dad was fascinated with this prospect. We had heard his many stories of the voyageurs and the *coureurs de bois:* their extraordinary strength, their endurance, their love of wilderness and songs and exploration. When he learned about

François Beaulieu, he dug up some of his favourite Canadian history books to show us underlined passages about Mackenzie and his voyages. Afterward he lent me a dog-eared copy of Peter C. Newman's *A Company of Adventurers*.

But the story didn't end there. Dad continued:

"And after the explorations with Mackenzie were finished, François Beaulieu went back to Great Slave Lake and married a Native woman there. How about that?"

"Huh."

The woman's name was not recorded in the genealogy, but it was clear that she had been Native because there were no white women there at the time. I remember thinking, there it is: evidence, of a circumstantial sort. This nameless ghost woman, my grandmother five or six generations removed, was the rumoured denizen of our family's woodpile. But we knew nothing about her except that she must have been Cree or Dene. She was just a space on a genealogy chart, a blank spot in the family, a race instead of a name. And she was so far back in the family tree that learning about her was little more than a curiosity to me.

It was different, though, to see a report in the newspaper about Dad's Metis heritage. He must have been referring to our nameless great-grandmother when the reporter took it as an affirmation of Metis identity.

Meanwhile, as I learned about this article and wondered what to make of its statements, the blockade continued. The publicity subsided after the first month or so, once the media decided that it wasn't likely to turn violent. But the protest continued. The RCMP waited. And Dad and the other sawmill people kept negotiating with the blockaders. I don't know exactly what Dad knew about the RCMP presence and the possibility of militaristic tactics on the part of the protestors, but I think he was still very worried. He must have had a sense that the outcome of this standoff would have repercussions in Meadow Lake for a long time afterward. And the longer it lasted, the more likely it was that something could go wrong.

Then, on July 1, the RCMP stormed the barricade and arrested dozens of protestors for trespassing. None of the threatened violence occurred during the arrests, though the protestors were obviously alarmed to be dragged away and thrown in jail. The arrests didn't even make national news; in fact there were hardly any media reports at all. I learned about the happenings from Mom and Dad when they phoned a few days later to wish me a happy birthday. I could hear the relief in their voices, though Dad was still worried that another protest would start up.

"It's over but it's not over," he said.

About a week after my birthday I got another phone call from Mom. She sounded too upbeat, too happy. She forgot to ask about the weather.

"I didn't want to say anything earlier because I didn't want to worry you," she said.

"About what?"

"Everything's fine now. Dad had a bit of a—heart problem last week. They took him down to Saskatoon on Tuesday and we came back up on Saturday. They're doing more tests, but he feels fine now. He just has to learn to take it easy."

The blockade had almost killed my father. That was what I thought and what I knew Mom was thinking. But after the initial wave of fear, another disturbing thought occurred to me. They hadn't told me about it. They had kept this all a secret from me, as I went about my daily routine in Toronto, studying, writing, wandering in Kensington Market. Why?

I knew it was because I was so far away. If I had been closer, someone would have told me. And I could have done something, could have come up for a visit or at least have sent a letter or made a phone call. But Dad had decided I was too far away to do anything, so it was better not to tell me.

At that moment, the distance came to have new meaning. I thought back to the week I had just lived, not knowing. A false week. I had started reading a novel called *The Dead Father*. After the phone call I put that novel back on the shelf and never opened it again.

Dad himself was less concerned about all this than the rest of us.

"How you feeling, Dad?" I asked him when Mom put him on the phone.

"Oh, fine." His breathing, a rush of nostril air. "Just a little blockage. It took care of itself. Then they put me on this crazy bike with wires stuck on me everywhere, and *that* damn near did me in. But I'm fine now. We're going golfing tomorrow."

That was the end of the story. I never knew what else I had missed: the pain, the fear, the worry. By the time I learned about it, it had already been erased.

Dad never admitted that he'd had a heart attack. He always referred to it as his "blockage," as if he thought some renegade faction of his body had been staging a protest.

We shared a playground,
a classroom, a town.

REMEMBERING CLAYTON

Less than a year after the blockade, Meadow Lake was in the news again, but this time I got no advance warning. The first thing I heard was a familiar name on the radio— a name that didn't belong there, a name from my childhood. I was living in Saskatoon again by this time, making my first concerted effort at full-time writing, and I used to leave the radio on in the other room while I wrote, to trick myself into thinking I wasn't alone. Usually it was just on the edge of intelligibility, a pleasant droning in the background, a patter of simulated companionship. But sometimes, despite my concentration on the writing, I heard bits of conversation, song lyrics, news highlights. On the afternoon I'm thinking of now, I heard only that name, one that was so out of place on the national airwaves that I didn't really register it for several seconds, and I didn't walk out to the other room for another half a minute. By that time the news piece was over, and I was left wondering why they were talking about Clayton Matchee, the skinny Native kid who had clung to the outskirts of my social group in Meadow Lake for years. Clayton had done well for him-self against the odds, had got married and had landed a good job with the army. What had happened to him, that he would make the national news?

I found out in the next broadcast. The announcer said that Master Corporal Clayton Matchee of the Fifth Airborne Division had been found hanging by a bootlace in a prison cell at the Canadian Forces peacekeeping base at Belet Huen, Somalia. He had been evacuated to a medical facility in that country but was expected to be returned to Canada for further treatment. Investigations had begun into the circumstances surrounding his injury.

As I listened, a slow tremor passed through my cluttered living room, like when distant bombs used to shake the ground at our cabin. I knew suddenly that on the edges of my happy childhood there had always been something else, some ominous possibility that would only become manifest when each of us went out into the world. I remembered the giggly eight-year-old I had played hockey against, the smart-ass kid in junior high school. Clayton had never been exactly my friend, but I had known him for many years, and his family was famous in Meadow Lake. He was the grandson of the Flying Dust Nation's most illustrious and long-lived hereditary chief, Gregoire Matchee. There was even a place called Matchee east of Meadow Lake, named after Chief Gregoire.

The first news about Clayton was devastating enough, but of course it was only the beginning. In the following weeks and months, there were many more revelations. The information arrived in bursts from my relentless radio, each requiring a separate observance of shock, of horror. Eventually a story emerged of what had happened the day before

Clayton's injury. A Somali boy named Shidane Arone was apprehended by the peacekeepers after he entered the Canadian military compound at Belet Huen in search of food. The soldiers, one of whom was Master Corporal Clayton Matchee, held Arone under armed guard while they kicked him and beat him with a metal bar. His cries of pain and his pleas for mercy echoed across the compound, but no one intervened in the attack. Eventually the cruelty escalated even further: Arone's captors burned the soles of his feet with cigarettes, and they posed with his semiconscious body for trophy-hunter-style photographs. And after more than three hours of torture, they killed him.

It seems clear to me and to many others that the attack was racially motivated, that Shidane Arone was systematically dehumanized, tortured, and murdered not because he was an interloper in the military compound but because he was black. In the days before the murder, soldiers of the Airborne were heard calling the local Somalis "nig-nogs," and making jokes about hunting them as trophies. In this context, Arone became a scapegoat in an almost ritualistic act of racism, an act that was preserved on the film of Private Kyle Brown's camera and later published in several Canadian newspapers. Clayton was the main figure in many of those photographs, and because I knew this, I couldn't bring myself to look at them for a long time. I had shared a playground with him, and a classroom, and a town. It seemed impossible that he could be present at the scene of such monumental depravity. Yet he was.

Along with everyone else, I wondered: where did these actions come from?

Millions of dollars were spent trying to answer that question. After the reports, the testimonies, and the trials, a consensus seems to have emerged that the Canadian military—rife with racism, poor leadership, and morale problems—provided the catalyst for the soldiers' acts of brutality. I have no doubt that this is true. But it is not the whole story. Each of these soldiers came from somewhere before they joined the Airborne. I don't know about the other men, but I can't help remembering that Clayton had learned all about racism and power during his childhood and youth in Meadow Lake. To see him portrayed as the aggressor in a racist attack is like the fulfillment of some nightmare prophecy. It makes no sense, and yet there is a murky symmetry to it that makes me think that racism—in Meadow Lake and elsewhere—is even more insidious than I had ever imagined.

I wish I could ask Clayton what he was doing there, but that's impossible now. He has never recovered from the injuries he sustained in the prison cell. It was ruled an attempted suicide and was interpreted by some as an admission of guilt, but no one really knows how it happened or what it might have meant. All we know is that the prison guards cut him down before the bootlace had finished its job, and since that time, Clayton has been one of the undead. He remains in a state of brain-damaged limbo, suspended between this world and the next, between guilty and innocent. He is unable to speak coherently, unable to understand the consequences of his actions, unfit to stand trial. And as the inquiries and the courts martial made their various reports, he became the *tabula rasa* upon which much of the blame was written. Some of the other soldiers testified that he was the instigator of the attack, the one who pushed it to its conclusion. One of the courts martial identified Clayton as "the main perpetrator" of the crimes against Shidane Arone. Everyone else has made their explanations, and to a large degree, Clayton *is* the explanation. But he will never be able to do any explaining of his own, and he will never be tried in a court of law to determine the true extent of his culpability.

Clayton's silence has been weighing on me almost as much as the possibility of his guilt. I know I can't speak for him here. I'm not trying to vindicate him, or to make excuses, or to cast blame. I only want to understand, even in the most rudimentary way, how he could have taken part in the crime that left a boy dead and a world in shock. I do believe that he was caught up in something larger than himself, something that belongs not only to the military but also to the culture in which he was raised. I can see something of this in the reaction to the initial publicity back home in Meadow Lake. Some townspeople were stunned to hear the news, and others were angry at Clayton for bringing shame upon the town. There were a few people, mostly from the Native community, who spoke in Clayton's defence early on, saying that he was not the kind of person who would willingly take part in such activities, and reminding everyone that none of the allegations had been proven. But there were also some people who claimed to have been expecting it. "I knew he'd fuck things up somehow," they said. They had been surprised earlier when Clayton seemed to be making something of himself, and now they were almost comforted to learn that it wasn't true after all.

But I understood that this was not just a character judgment. What they meant was: he's not an exception after all;

he's just like all the other Indians. They wanted to see him as a born savage, a symbol of his people.

Later, when the Somalia photographs were published, that sentiment was expressed even more blatantly. Clayton's family in Meadow Lake received a barrage of anonymous death threats and hate mail. His father, Leon Matchee, described the attacks as "mostly a lot of swear words and very poorly written—'Indian, welfare bum, you deserve to die, you should be dead.'" It is instructive to compare these comments with the racist aspects of the crime Clayton was accused of.

Nothing I knew about Clayton could have led me to expect that he might be involved in anything like the Somalia scandal. As a boy, he was not extraordinarily violent or depraved or dissolute—not a monster in the making, as some people now might want to believe. He got into trouble regularly, and he was known to be someone you didn't want to pick a fight with, but I never saw him do anything cruel. What I remember most about him was that he wanted desperately to fit in. I could sense this in the way he haunted the hallways at recess, listening in on the conversations of more popular kids, tossing in comments from the sidelines.

Clayton was different from Billy Tootoosis and the Fiddler boys, who sometimes seemed to enjoy intimidation. He didn't belong to a gang, and as far as I can remember he didn't make a pastime out of terrorizing the white kids. I think it was because he wanted to be one of them. He *was* part white, after all—though none of the white kids knew this at the time. His mother was of mixed European ancestry, and she had moved out to the Flying Dust Reserve only after marrying Leon Matchee. But Clayton's skin was as dark as any Native person's, and he lived on the reserve, so nobody in Meadow Lake bothered to think of him as anything other than an Indian. And so he was treated like they were.

There *were* exceptions to the town's division between Native and white roles, but they were always invoked with the knowledge that they were exceptions. Gilbert Lachance was welcomed among the white kids because he was a talented athlete, and Frankie Caplette was tolerated because his parents had given him a motorcycle for his thirteenth birthday. But Clayton was not an exception, at least not then, much as he may have wanted to be. It was only years later, when he married a white woman from town and got a good job in the army, that people started thinking of him as an exception.

It must have been hard work, being an exception. Even for those Native kids who *were* welcomed into the white crowd, the trial was never over. If they made the football or basketball or volleyball teams, they crossed over into a certain kind of respectability in school, but they always had to continue proving themselves, and the price of such proof was often horrendous. I remember on the volleyball team in high school there was an aboriginal guy named Gary. He was a strong power-hitter and a pretty fast digger in the backcourt, but no one looked up to him. He was treated as the team's jester instead, and he played along with this role, perhaps realizing that it was the only one he was likely to get. We called him Tomahawk, and he went along with it. If he wanted to feel like part of the team, he had no choice in the matter. At practice someone would say, "Hey, Tomahawk, you scalping bastard, you," and he would laugh with the rest of us. Sometimes he would brandish an imaginary tomahawk or give a ridiculous war whoop, as if he could efface his native-ness by ridiculing it like everyone else did. After a while he began making racist comments about the Indians on the teams we played against. He ranted about them, stringing together curses and racist insults that he had certainly learned the hard way. This was the zenith of Gary's belonging. When he had learned to act out the racism of the team and project it onto our rivals, he was as close to being an honorary white man as he was going to get. Gary had learned two things in his search for approval: that whiteness is power, and that the way to become white is to be a racist.

I don't remember exactly what terrible things we said to Clayton, but I know he got the same treatment as every other dark-skinned person in the school. Nobody was immune to it. Even the tough kids like Clayton were subject to taunting and verbal abuse, especially at school, when the perpetrators could run to the teachers for protection whenever necessary. This was probably one of the reasons Clayton was always getting into trouble. And even when he wasn't being taunted himself, he would have witnessed the attacks on other Native kids. Seeing all this, day after day, would be enough to make any-one wish they were white, just as a matter of survival.

Clayton left school after grade ten, and I lost track of him for a few years. I can't say that I thought about him much. By the time I finished high school I heard he was working in the bush, cutting trees or operating a skidder. Two

years after that I bumped into him and his friend Jeremy on
the banks of the Green River, where they were fishing and I
was looking for a spot to fish. They were bigger and more
muscular now, but essentially they hadn't changed since grade
nine: still goofy and hyperactive, still fond of shoulder-
punching and fart jokes. They didn't ask me anything about
myself, but when I inquired about the fishing Jeremy showed
me a string of walleye laid out in the grass beside half a dozen
empty bottles of beer. Clayton started razzing him about the
little pickerel he had kept. I remember his laugh: a high-
pitched, theatrical giggle that sounded like someone was
tickling him. The two of them were wrestling over the last
beer when I left, so none of us said goodbye.

That was the last time I ever heard from Clayton. His
unlikely changes occurred shortly after. He married the
daughter of a respected family in Meadow Lake and then he
enlisted in the Canadian Armed Forces. It's hard to believe
that any Native people would willingly join the same institu-
tion that the government has repeatedly used to repress
indigenous people in this country. But many other Native
people before Clayton and after him also joined the army,
simply because it's a respectable job, a place where their skills
and dedication might be valued. Perhaps no other employer
will give them a chance. In any case, Clayton was very
successful as a soldier, so perhaps he felt he had found his
vocation. Still, I wonder what he thought in the summer of
1990, when the Canadian government sent troops to the bar-
ricades at Oka, to put down an Indian uprising once again.
Clayton's own reserve and his own army division weren't
involved, so maybe he didn't worry much about it. He might

have had other things to think about, because the Third Airborne Division, in which he was stationed, was a hotbed of racist activities.

Any reports about Clayton's behaviour in the army during his pre-Somalia days are probably tainted by what happened later, so it's difficult to know exactly what role he played in the Airborne's now-notorious racism. Official and unofficial investigations have revealed that several members of the division openly espoused neo-Nazi and white supremacist beliefs. There were horrifyingly degrading initiation rituals, during which visible minorities were singled out for the most extreme humiliation. They were beaten, insulted, smeared with excrement. If they wanted to be part of the group, they had to suffer this abuse without complaint. Once they had gotten through the ordeal, they were accepted into the group—and a sign of their belonging was that, in the next year's initiation, they got to be the aggressors.

Clayton must have undergone an initiation of this sort. It's the nature of these rituals that no exceptions are allowed. There is no record of his initiation, nor of course his reaction to it, but I imagine the ordeal itself wouldn't have come as a surprise to him. He would have already known the rules from his youth in Meadow Lake, where almost every sports team practised some variation of this vicious rite of passage. I can only speculate about this, but it seems probable that during his time in the Airborne, Clayton learned something very similar to what my teammate Gary had learned on the Carpenter High School volleyball team: that in order to be accepted by a racist white majority, he had to adopt their prejudices himself.

There is some evidence that Clayton was indeed accepted among his peers at the Airborne, but he didn't have to play the role of the jester like Gary had done. In fact, he was something of a leader. He was promoted rapidly, to corporal and then to master corporal. At the same time, his once-skinny body began to fill out, and he became an imposing man: muscular, self-assured, seemingly fearless. There are rumours that other soldiers in the division were afraid of him because of his strength and his ferocity during training exercises. This is one explanation of how Clayton came to be the instigator of the attack on Shidane Arone. The other participants said they were scared to stop him.

I fear him too, now that I have seen him in the terrible photographs, the ones that caused a national furor when they were published in Canadian newspapers. I couldn't bring myself to look at them then, but years later I realized I had to face them if I was to come to terms with Clayton's actions. I looked them up on microfilm, clenching my teeth as I scrolled back through the myriad calamities of yesterday's news. There they were. The scratches and distortions of the microfilm did nothing to disguise the brutality of the images. I looked away, at the cool orderliness of the library reading room, then back into Clayton's face. It was almost impossible to reconcile those vicious poses with my memories of the boy I knew, and yet it *was* unmistakably Clayton, there at the scene of horror.

In one of the photos he points with his index finger at Shidane Arone's swollen and bloodied head, perhaps mimicking a handgun, or maybe just pointing out the damage that has already been done. On Clayton's face is a smirk, a cocksure expression, perhaps even a show of pride. In the most horrific of the published photographs, Shidane Arone leans forward, bound by two thick ropes, blindfolded with a piece of plaid cloth that drapes from his head onto his right shoulder. The cloth is Clayton's shirt, which he has removed sometime during the torture. Clayton stands above Arone's shoulders, almost riding on the prisoner's back, and he holds a long metal bar between his outstretched hands. He has forced the bar into Shidane Arone's bloodied mouth, and now he holds it there, looking up into the camera with an expression that is a mixture of solemnity, questioning, and pride. His face is like that of a small boy looking up at his father for affirmation. His bare chest almost touches the back of Arone's head, and the powerful muscles of his arms and shoulders are outlined against the white of his pants. It's a pure display of strength, like the poses in bodybuilding magazines. But something else is also on display here, something that Clayton had usually taken pains to cover up.

Look, he seems to be saying. *My skin is lighter than his.*

Almost two years after the murder of Shidane Arone, Clayton returned home—or as near to home as institutional facilities would allow. He is now a patient in the mental hospital in North Battleford, ninety miles south of Meadow Lake. It's the place we all used to joke about as kids: the loony bin, the funny farm, the zoo. The way we talked, half of our friends were either recent escapees or were soon to be patients. If we had believed that any of us might actually end up there, the jokes wouldn't have been so funny.

Even as it was, the very idea of the place made me queasy. Our grade seven teacher once told us about a patient he had seen there: a teenage boy who had sniffed so much gasoline that he became a vegetable. This boy's mind, the teacher said, was so completely vacant that all he could do, day in and day out, was stare up into the corner of his room. The only thing the staff could do for him was to hang a balloon up there in the corner so he had something pretty to look at. Every few days, as a favour to him, they changed the colour of the balloon.

In my imagination, Clayton became that lost boy. I often thought of him up there, alone in his room, sitting in a low vinyl chair with his head leaned back against the wall, his mouth partly open. I pictured a whole ward full of people like him, and dozens of other silent patients shuffling in the halls, trembling to the rhythms of their medications.

I knew that Clayton was no longer Clayton. But still there was a body that occupied his space in the world, and his family called that body by his name. So did the nurses in the hospital. I supposed they didn't hold his reputation against him. To them, he would be just another body to shepherd through the cycles of eating, shitting, sleeping, walking.

The official reports were never very clear about Clayton's level of mental functioning. Sometimes I wondered: does he have any memory of Somalia? Of his wife and daughter? His hometown? Can he express love, or remorse, or anger? Does he dream?

He had been up there in his room for years already when I went to visit him. I went there not to ask questions but simply to look into his face, to remind myself that part of him, at least, lived on. There was also something I felt I had to tell him about myself, something he might have found funny or tragic or ironic if he could understand me. So one September afternoon when I was visiting Meadow Lake, I drove down to the outskirts of North Battleford, where the Mental Health Centre looks out on the magnificent Battle River valley. It was a far more beautiful place than any of my imaginings had prepared me for.

"I'm here to visit someone I used to know," I said at the front desk where two nurses were sorting through a sheaf of papers. "Clayton Matchee."

Both of them stopped, looked at each other. I wondered if such a request was unusual, or if Clayton still received death threats even now.

"What relation are you?" the nearest one asked.

"We went to school together in Meadow Lake."

She informed me that Clayton had a restricted visitors' list, but still, they would see what they could do. I was told to fill out a form indicating my connection to the patient, and then one of the nurses made a cryptic phone call while the other one disappeared down the corridor.

I waited for a long time in that hallway. Patients and nurses and doctors strode past, each of them glancing at me appraisingly, as if to decide what category I belonged in. Somewhere, probably only a few feet away, Clayton would be waiting. I tried not to think about what he had once been; tried to focus on what he might be now, though that wasn't much of a diversion. By the time I saw the nurse coming back down the hallway I could feel my pulse in my palms, my ears.

But they didn't let me in. She was shaking her head as she approached, and the apprehension had almost drained out of me when she finally spoke.

"I'm sorry," she said. "He doesn't remember you."

My great-grandparents, John and Eleanor Beaulieu.

BORN *in* FORGET

What I wanted to tell Clayton was that I had learned some-thing surprising about myself in the time since he had gone to Somalia. My grandmother, Marie Clemence, had died in 1991, and in the following few years the family had begun to talk about her history. The information came gradually, and at first it took the form of nuances, unfinished sentences, sug-gestions. Eventually one of my aunts came out and told me—almost nonchalantly, in the midst of other family reminis-cences while we were cleaning raspberries from the garden—that her mother had been of mixed Native ancestry: that she was Metis.

"You mean from the voyageur's wife?" I said, thinking back to what Dad had told me about our ancestor François Beaulieu in the eighteenth century.

"Oh no, they were all Metis," she said. "Her mom and dad both, and all their families way back." She went on to tell me that Grandma had learned Cree as a young girl, and that our ancestors had been part of the Red River Settlement.

As I listened I felt like I was standing on muskeg. *Where do I come from?* The story I had been telling myself all my life was incomplete, incorrect. Norway, France, Germany, my mother's belly, my hometown, yes. But Indian? How could that be?

"Mom's mother was born in a place called Forget," my aunt added, "and one time I asked Aunt Josephine how come my grandma was born so far away from Ituna, and she said, 'Oh, they were on a buffalo hunt.'"

My aunt said all this as if it were a historical curiosity rather than something that might have a real effect on Grandma's descendants. But to me, having grown up in a community that was hypersensitive about the divisions between Native and white, this information was unsettling, to say the least. What did it mean about me? I remembered the Fiddler boys chasing me through town, yelling in Cree. At the time we all thought we knew what sides we were on.

So *Grandma* was the Indian in the woodpile, the one my family had been speculating about all those years. I had known that her second husband (not my grandfather) was Metis, but somehow I had never considered that Grandma herself might be Metis as well. *I* was white, after all, and so were my parents. Everyone in Meadow Lake would have said so.

Grandma would have probably said so too. I had never heard her deny having Native ancestry, but I had certainly never heard her proclaim it either, and I think the silence of her children on the subject indicated that she was not interested in spreading the news. This is not at all surprising, given the prejudices against Native people and against the Metis in particular during her lifetime. She was born within a generation of Louis Riel's execution, and raised in an era when Metis people had many reasons to disguise their heritage if they could. For a long time after the North West Rebellion, to be Metis was to be considered traitorous, untrustworthy, savage. Officially, the government treated the Metis as if they didn't exist, saying that they should choose to be either white or Indian and should deal with the government as one or the other.

Many Metis were pushed off their lands after the rebellion, by soldiers and then by settlers. After this, most of them had absolutely nothing: no home, no pride, no status in the eyes of the nation. They were at the absolute bottom of the social scale, lower even than the Status Indians, who had at least some land and the dubious honour of treaties. In the great dispersal of Metis people after the rebellion, it was no wonder that many of them chose to suppress their Metis identity when they moved to new places. Passing as white was a survival technique; those who couldn't do that would often try to pass as Cree. The result was that generations of Metis were born into a vast canyon of forgetting.

Now that we have been shaken into remembering, everyone in my family has dealt with the knowledge in their own ways. Some would rather not acknowledge it at all, while others see that the Native heritage is there, but they don't see how it matters, why it should make any difference to who and what we are now. A few have gone so far as to claim themselves as Metis and to announce this publicly by becoming official members of provincial Metis associations. It is a source of great controversy in the family, and one measure of the strength of this controversy is the fact that it is still seldom discussed.

For me, the knowledge did matter. I started to wonder if I really was the person I had thought I was, if I really belonged where I had always assumed I did. I found myself in a between-space, a location that the logic of Meadow Lake didn't allow. It was impossible to be both a Native person and a non-Native person; the two notions were mutually exclusive.

I didn't discuss this quandary much at first. I thought most people would scoff at any claims I might make regarding aboriginal identity—and I wouldn't really have blamed them for scoffing. I felt a certain amount of guilt about the fact that this Native heritage had been hidden for so long, and about the possibility that I had unknowingly benefited from that secrecy. I had never been subject to discrimination on the basis of my hidden Native ancestry. Now that it was becoming more socially acceptable to be a Native person—at least in the cities where I had lived for several years—I wondered if it was hypocritical to announce this discovery about myself. But to keep that aspect of my family's past a secret also felt wrong, was a perpetuation of the racial divide that had existed for so long in Meadow Lake and across the continent.

I also wondered what Native people would think about such claims. For generations, they have been the focal points of impersonation schemes by Europeans. Grey Owl is the most famous example of this, but there have been many other non-Native people who have tried to supplement some missing aspect of themselves by attempting to become Native. The last thing I wanted was to be seen as one of these contemporary Grey Owls, who often unwittingly cause offence to the very people they seek to emulate.

As some other members of my family began to go public with our family secret, though, I started to feel a little more comfortable with it. One of my cousins informed me that she had joined the Manitoba Metis Federation, and my uncle Vic started to become active in Saskatchewan Metis politics. Most of my friends in Toronto were quite excited to learn about my Metis ancestry. Some even treated me with a certain amount of awe, perhaps because they had only met a precious few real Native people, or because they believed that being aboriginal was somehow inherently valuable. Others were confused by the contrast between my appearance and the revelation of my background. I don't "look Native," if there is such a look. Nonetheless, some of my acquaintances claimed to be able to see it in my cheekbones.

Once I had mentioned the family secret to a few people, it began to take on a life of its own, and I started to wish I had kept it to myself. People seemed to be unable or unwilling to accept the idea that I could be Metis *and* Norwegian *and* German *and* French. For some of them I became simply "the Native guy," while others insisted, "Yeah, but you're white; I mean, look at you." At the same time I was, as always, privy to racist comments against Indians, made by people who assumed I had no connection to them.

I never did talk to Dad about all this, though I heard him acknowledge his Metis ancestry a few times after the fact became established in the family. I didn't ask him how long he had known about Grandma's origins, or whether he had always known. I didn't ask if he had ever thought that he was keeping a secret or that others in the family were keeping one from him. I wondered if he felt the same kind of destabilization that I felt, the same sense of self-division. He had lived in Meadow Lake for longer than I had; he must have sensed the weight of the community's contradictions within himself. Did he think of himself as Metis, or as white, or as something else—a hybrid of a hybrid? I wanted to know all this, but the subject had such an aura of taboo about it that I couldn't bring myself to ask him.

A few years later, when I ended up being called "a Metis writer" in the national media, I realized that I had to think seriously about the ways I would advertise my identity. And the more I thought about it, the more it became clear to me that I simply don't *feel* like I am exclusively an aboriginal person. I have some Metis ancestry, and I have been raised among many Native people, but I didn't grow up with the sense that I was one, and I have never learned their cultures from the perspective of an insider. I feel closely connected to Native people, and particularly to the Metis, but it doesn't seem quite right to claim that I am one. I am instead a little of this and a little of that; a child of the heterogeneous multitudes. I come from half the globe, and I come from Meadow Lake.

My family situation is far from unique. Demographers have estimated that there are hundreds of thousands of Canadians who have some Native ancestry but either don't know it or don't care to admit it. This can be explained by the historic stigma attached to racial difference in this country, but in addition, I think, we are still largely incapable of understanding and accepting hybridity here. So people are encouraged to cover up certain aspects of their lineage to conform to the generally accepted racial identities that are available to them.

In the mid-nineties in Saskatchewan there was a kind of experiment in racial self-definition. A Non-Status Metis man was charged with hunting out of season, and when he challenged this charge in the courts on the basis of aboriginal hunting rights, his initial conviction was overturned. This meant that from 1995 until 1997, when the conviction was reinstated in the Appeals Court, all Non-Status indigenous people were granted hunting and fishing rights in Saskatchewan. Anyone who could prove having Metis ancestry could hunt and fish whenever they wanted, without licences.

In Meadow Lake, hunting and fishing are serious pursuits, and this sudden bonanza in the regulations resulted in a virtual stampede for the Metis Association offices, where dozens of people went to proclaim and reinstate their indigenous heritage. At least one of my relatives participated in this sudden campaign for legitimation. All anyone needed was a "Metis card" to be able to hunt and fish without regard for the regulations. Hundreds of people in the district who had not advertised their indigenous status before were now announcing it publicly. There were plumbers, electricians, ranchers, construction workers—even some people I had gone to school with. It appeared that half the "white" people in town had at least some aboriginal lineage.

It's too bad that it took a judicial loophole, and a rather comical incentive, to expose this hidden aspect of Meadow Lake's population, but nonetheless it has had significant effects on the ways the townspeople think about each other. The most important thing it did was to obliterate any notion that there was an easily discernible racial divide in Meadow Lake. Many people who I had thought were white turned out to be not entirely white. Once they had made their family secrets public, the very ideas of pure whiteness and pure nativeness became suddenly improbable.

I think of this in relation to myself and Clayton Matchee. When we were growing up, people were considered either Native or white, and that distinction went a long way toward deciding what you were going to do in life. Clayton and I had been placed on different sides of the division. But the more I have learned about us, the more I see that the very idea of this division is a falsehood. I have gleaned all the benefits, while Clayton and many others have suffered devastating discrimination. What is the real difference between us?

I can see why people would want to pass. How much of what I now have—education, health, a decent self-image, a job—can be attributed to my grandmother's decision to live as a French woman instead of a Metis? I wonder if my father could have gone to university if people had known about his ancestry, and if my parents would even have met. Maybe Grandma knew that she was protecting her children from the arbitrary rules of a racist society when she raised them in the French way—her husband's way.

This was essentially what Clayton had wanted to do: protect himself by identifying with the powerful. But his skin always gave him away.

*Grandma Laliberte (Marie Clemence) with her first
husband, my grandfather Charles Julien Cariou.*

MARIE CLEMENCE

In all my life I had never wondered about where Grandma had come from; she was so imposing that it seemed she had always existed. I assumed that she was French, like her husband. She spoke the language at home and especially at church, and she spoke English with what I recognized as a French accent: a telltale nasality in her pronunciation of "no," a fluidity of sentence rhythms. She said "close the light" instead of "shut off the light," and she was given to francophone repetitions like "Vic, he went out to the store." I suppose this was all the evidence I needed.

I don't know to what extent Grandma cultivated this Frenchness, if at all. I wonder if she was consciously keeping her Metis past a secret, or if she had simply moved on to another way of thinking about herself. Perhaps she did still think of herself as Metis all along but saw no need to make an issue of it, to declare it repeatedly and publicly. It's hard to know whether there was ever really a secret at all.

Whatever the reason—secret or not—I simply wasn't told about Grandma's origins. I don't think her own children were directly told about it either, though I imagine at least the older ones would have seen some evidence in the behaviour and appearance of their maternal grandparents. There were of course the jokes about the woodpile, which indicated that someone knew something. I didn't know quite what to make of those jokes, but I sometimes pictured a cuckoldry scene set in the eighteenth or nineteenth century: a Native man huddling under a pile of split wood, with his buckskins half down, while my sturdy Frankish forefather strode blithely in his front door. It was strange how an anomaly in family appearance could occasion such absurdities. The only safe way to mention the possibility was in the context of a joke. But none of those jokes were ever told in Grandma's presence.

Grandma was a monumental figure in our lives, even though she moved away from Meadow Lake before I was born. She came for regular visits, especially after we had moved out to the farm. Even when she wasn't there, you could feel her presence whenever any of her children came to the house. She was a matriarch in the truest sense of the word: the centre and figurehead of an immense family, the seat of authority and love and judgment, the embodiment of female strength. She was not a sweet little old lady, and there was nothing feeble about her, even in her last years when she was confined to a wheelchair. She had an imperious, wilful disposition at times, an authority that manifested itself in the gleam of her fiercely intelligent, raptor-like black eyes. Most of her grandchildren—forty-seven in all—were afraid of her.

Grandma wasn't polite, at least not when she spoke to the kids. She said "Gimme." "Gimme those scissors, you," she would say while looming over the sewing machine, or "Gimme a little more soup, eh, be sure it's good and hot!"

"Gimme gimme never gets," we would sing to ourselves as we performed the demanded task.

Grandma could also be stubbornly judgmental, especially in matters of religion and morality. She was fiercely Catholic, and firmly held to the prejudices of her generation and her faith. Once when she was introduced to a new grandchild whose parents were not yet married, she said, "Let's see the little bastard, then." She continued to refer to the child as The Little Bastard until the day his parents were married.

There were many good reasons for Grandma's flinty character, however. She was a product of a life of almost unimaginable hardship, the kind of life that seems only possible in latter-day jokes about the Depression. She had given birth to fifteen children and raised them throughout the thirties and forties, much of that time as a widow, on a tiny farm at the edge of the Palliser Triangle. Dad's stories had always made his boyhood sound like fun, but I realize now that it was desperate much of the time. They dug seneca root and picked rocks and snared gophers to supplement their income, and they relied on the extended family for help. Grandma worked all day, virtually every day, washing and cooking and tending to the kids' various injuries and illnesses. I can hardly imagine a more severe, more taxing, more utterly hopeless and degrading way of life, but Grandma came through it all. I think that's where her sense of defiance, her proud demeanour, were galvanized. By the time I knew her, she had survived everything that the twentieth century could throw at her, and she was ready for more.

But Grandma was not simply a hardened woman. She was a sensualist, despite her fanatical Catholicism and her absurdly difficult life. She had a tremendous appetite for enjoyment. She loved fresh food from the garden and especially wild food gathered or hunted or fished from the nearby land and lakes. Blueberries and pickerel were her favourites, as they are mine. She pronounced the word *pickerel* with extraordinary relish. You could hear the rush of salivation in her consonants. She emphasized each syllable, refusing to reduce the word to "pick'rel" like the rest of us did.

With blueberries she was even more effusive. Her accent seemed to get stronger when she was faced with a patch of berries, or even when she recalled blueberries of the past. "Oh, my my my my," she would say, "loook at those beddies!" And she would lie down on her side, right in the middle of the patch, and proceed to pick them faster than all of us, moving slowly along the ground like a large gingham-clad combine, and she would eventually emerge from the underbrush with an overflowing ice-cream pail, stigmata of berry stains on her hands and her dress, and a brazenly purple tongue.

Whenever she ate blueberries she held them on her palm, lifted her hand up toward her lips as if preparing to blow someone a kiss, and then sucked them up into her mouth a few at a time with brief and resounding inhalations. I used to watch the berries disappearing by the magic of vacuum into Grandma's soft, nearly lipless mouth. When she chewed, a glow of ecstasy transformed her usually taciturn features.

She also loved music, particularly her own music, which she played with mischievous delight on the harmonica. Before she played, she always took her teeth out and hid them in a pocket of her dress. Then she cupped her hands around her mouth, and hesitated, like a teenager embarrassed by orthodontics. She leaned forward, inhaled, and glanced quickly up at her audience with a distinct hint of devilment in her dark eyes. Anyone watching from a distance would have sworn that she was laughing into her hands. But instead of laughter there came music: slides and squawks and glissandos and rhythmic train sounds chuffing along in the background. I was captivated. Her body weaved back and forth with the rhythm, and sometimes her eyes would close—but then they would flash open, full of playfulness. At the end of a song, the hands always fell away from her mouth, and she favoured us with a toothless grin.

I didn't recognize any of Grandma's songs, but I suppose they were traditional ones. She said she had learned to play as a girl. That was the only reference to her childhood I ever heard her make.

I was such a dedicated fan of Grandma's music that on my seventh birthday she gave me a harmonica of my own, a small red and silver one with Pocket Pal engraved on the top. She didn't see me often enough to teach me any of her songs, but she gave me brief lessons on the instrument, showing me how to cradle it over my mouth, how to make a V shape with my tongue so I could play a single clean note. I longed to be able to play like Grandma, but I never actually learned. Instead I made a lot of noise. I slid the instrument back and forth across my mouth like the platen of a typewriter, inhaling and exhaling a flurry of notes. Sometimes when my friends came over I would pretend to play a song, mimicking Grandma's posture, her trick with the eyes, her finale smile. I played random sounds and hoped no one would notice.

Grandma had the most vivid and entertaining dreams of anyone I've ever known, and she was always willing to recount them. Whenever she was visiting we would rush downstairs each morning to ask her what she had dreamed. Most of them were about the Depression in one way or another—hunger dreams, dust dreams, grasshopper dreams—though sometimes the Pope or some other famous personage would make an appearance. Once she told us about going blueberry picking with her kids back on the farm in Ituna and looking up from the berry patch to see the neighbour's bull staring down at her.

"Janecki's bull, with those great big horns, you know, and looking at me with that look bulls get"—she glowered at us and flared her nostrils—"and his front feet stomp-stomping the ground. And I yelled at him, 'Gwan,' I said, 'gwan lay down!' but he kept following, brushing his chin on the ground, flicking his tail. And I said to the kids, 'You kids get to the other side of that fence!'"

It was enough to give me my own nightmares. Luckily there were other dreams that were more in the comic mode. The most famous of these was what became known as the Trudeau Dream. We loved it so much that we often asked her to repeat it, for our own enjoyment as well as for the entertainment of visiting friends and relatives.

She was always willing to retell it if we pleaded with her long enough

"My my my," she would say, shaking her head. "I dreamt we were all back at the farm in Ituna, and Pierre Trudeau came for a visit. But it was him how he is *now*, as prime minister. Leo saw him coming in a Bennett buggy, you know, an old Model T car with two horses in front pulling, because nobody could afford the fuel. And Leo, he called out, 'Trudeau's coming! Trudeau's coming!' and I was standing in the kitchen and I said to myself, 'Oh nooo, it's breakfast time and there's nothing to feed him.' Because it was the Depression.

"I was so embarrassed, but I had to do something so I said to Charlie and your dad, 'You boys run out to the chickens and see if there's any more eggs.' And just when Trudeau's horses turned at the lane, the boys came in with half a dozen eggs between them. A miracle!

"So we invited the prime minister in, and oh he was friendly, and he didn't say anything about our dirty old farmhouse, you know, with the broken windows and the space under the door. But he went to sit down and I said, 'Not *that* chair, it only has three legs!' And then I fried up all the eggs and told Ginger, 'You take Mr. Trudeau his eggs now.' But when she walked to the table, one of the eggs slipped right off the plate, and when it hit the floor it slipped through a great big hole in the floorboards and disappeared.

"Well, I was so darn embarrassed I woke myself up."

She laughed at her dreams most of the time, even the frightening ones. But there were other dreams that she never told us kids about, ones that we learned about only by listening in on our aunts and uncles. It was known in the family that Grandma had a kind of second sight. Whenever anyone in the family died, she dreamed of flowers. One of her kids would phone her to give her the news and she would already know, or at least partly know. Sometimes she phoned them first. "Something happened. Who was it?" I remember once hearing the aunts and uncles whispering to each other, "She had the flower dream." Then they were silent, wondering who it was.

Dad was not the type to believe in such things, but he made an exception in his mother's case. He had seen the truth of it, and he told us the story many times. One night when he was only nine or ten, Grandma had had a dream in which her sister Josephine appeared at the foot of her bed and spoke to her, telling her not to worry, asking Grandma to pray for her. Grandma got out of bed immediately after the dream and woke up Dad and Uncle Leo.

"You boys gwan over to Aunt Josephine's right now," she said. "Something's happened."

And they stumbled across the field in the pre-dawn chill to find that Aunt Josephine had died in her sleep.

Maybe Grandma's clairvoyance also had something to do with her skill at games of chance. She loved cards and casinos and raffles and lotteries—and especially bingo. Her card games were not parlour games like bridge or hearts or kaiser; they were the backroom games, the rumpus-room games: cribbage, Rummoli, thirty-one. She played thirty-one with such intensity that if she was planning to knock (a sign that everyone else has only one more draw to form a respectable hand), she would form a fist on the tabletop well in advance.

The only places she ever travelled, outside of Canada, were the Holy Land and Reno. Both of these trips could be considered pilgrimages. It must be said, however, that she visited Reno many times and Jerusalem only once. She had always wanted to go to Israel, and in 1978, when she was eighty-one years old, her children got together enough money to send her there. She returned with stories of riding on a camel (which had tried to bite her), going to Bethlehem, bathing in the Sea of Galilee. It must have been an outlandish experience for someone of her generation and experience, to travel halfway across the world. But I suppose she had gained a ready familiarity with the place through her lifetime of devotion to the Bible. When she returned home, she brought hand-carved wooden rosaries for us kids, and for Dad a magnetized hood ornament of the Virgin Mary encased in glass.

Grandma spent significantly more time over the years in the American Babylon than she did in Jerusalem—but when she came back from Reno she usually didn't bring us anything, either because she had lost all her money playing micro-stakes keno and kingo and bingo or because she didn't want to encourage us to follow her example. Of course there was already plenty of such encouragement whenever she came to visit us. She always had a bag of plastic winecoloured bingo chips in her purse, and usually also a white bingo dabber with 777 Bingo King marked on the side in blood-red ink. We were always rummaging in her purse, hoping to find the dabber and stamp it on sheets of scrap paper, or preferably on each other. We dug past the harmonica in its green leather box, past the combs, the hairpins, the lottery tickets, in search of the dabber or—what we thought of as second-best—her bottle of fruit punch–flavoured Tums, which we devoured like candy. Considering that we were afraid of her, we took surprising liberties with her purse.

Grandma went "bingoing" nearly as regularly as she attended mass. The church-basement bingos were as entertaining to her as the big-jackpot extravaganzas that were held at the civic centre or the hockey arena. Sometimes we were allowed to come along and sit in the noisy, smoke-fogged rooms, where we watched the miracle of the bingo machine: its ping-pong balls frothing like an erupting volcano, and one of them neatly appearing at the end of the machine's nozzle, like a fresh-laid egg. When we were a little older, Glenn and I were allowed to have one card between us, and we wrestled with the chips so much that we usually ended up dumping the whole works on the floor. I remember the different games: straight line, diagonal, L, X, super-blackout. We always got the wrong one at the wrong time.

At the bingo halls, the Native people clearly outnumbered the whites, and they seemed so much more comfortable than at church or in the streets. They teased each other, told jokes, guffawed with wide-open mouths. The kids played tag at the back of the hall, crawled under the paper-clad tables, clambered over the adults' laps without ever displacing a bingo chip. Here they were free, happy, hilarious. I could see that for most of them—as for Grandma—the attraction of bingo was social rather than monetary. Grandma laughed along with everybody else, and so did I. This was the one public occasion when I wasn't afraid of Indians.

A few times we went to a drive in bingo, held in the parking lot of the civic centre, at the edge of the stampede grounds. Everyone sat in their cars with their radios tuned to the local station, and volunteers walked the lot selling bingo cards from window to window. You were supposed to arrange your cards on your lap, and if you managed to match the designated pattern of the moment—X, L, etc.—you had to honk your horn instead of yelling bingo. I remember sitting there in our old blue Plymouth Fury with Mom and Dad and Grandma, waiting to hammer on that horn. But we weren't lucky that time, so I was left to fidget in the front seat between Mom and Dad. Now that I think of it, I never saw Grandma or anyone else in our family get lucky at bingo.

Dad, too, had an intimate connection to bingo, though he didn't play very often and, as far as I know, he never won. For a few years he had a more prominent role than the players. Through his association with the Lions Club in Meadow Lake, he became the designated bingo caller for all the big-jackpot games in town, the ones that came only twice a year and advertised up to fifty thousand dollars in prizes. Each "Bingo Weekend" the population of Meadow Lake tripled, as hundreds of people flooded into town from all the northern communities. When I worked at Kentucky Fried Chicken in high school, we used to dread the "bingo rush," which usually hit us at ten thirty on a bingo night. The bingo rush meant endless streams of customers who ordered their chicken by the bucket.

Bingo was and is a big deal in Meadow Lake, and Dad was the most visible part of the biggest bingos in town. This is probably why he was so well known in the surrounding districts. All the players knew him by name. He told them bad jokes, encouraged them when their luck was down, built up the excitement with his patter when the jackpot was coming close. He added his own cigarillo smog to the heavily polluted atmosphere of the hockey rink, where scores of tables were arranged on the ice surface, and every table contained a dozen heaping ashtrays.

The northerners called him Raymond for some reason, instead of Ray. Perhaps it was a gesture of respect. He was after all the one who reached down to the magic machine and allowed it to lay its golden egg in his hand. He became the voice of fate, the bearer of luck—good and bad. They would plead with him sometimes.

"Raymon! Raymon! I need a O sixta-seven."

"Help me win that truck, Raymon, my ol' one's no damn good."

"Ayah, Raymon, don't call any more a them N's!"

He was in his glory. I don't think Grandma ever saw him up there, but if she had, she would have been thrilled.

Grandma passed on her bingo obsession to her youngest son, Vic. Uncle Vic was hooked on bingo for as far back as I can remember. He used to go with her to the bingos around Meadow Lake, and if he could afford it he would play even more cards than she did. I remember him leaning on the makeshift plywood tables of the civic centre, two cigarettes going in the ashtray, coffee stains on his grid of nine cards, piles of bingo chips arranged neatly along the left and right sides of the cards. He always had time to trade bullshit with the people sitting around him, and to watch their cards as well as his own. Whenever he was within one or two numbers of a bingo he would nudge me with his elbow and point portentously at the empty squares, lifting his eyebrows and his glasses along with them. He never hit the magic combination when I was there to witness, but I heard the stories of his winnings many times. He won a washer and dryer once, and promptly sold them to his girlfriend. A few years later he borrowed some money from Dad and Uncle Charlie to buy a few bingo tickets, and he won a thousand dollars—so he divided his winnings with his brothers. Another time he won more than three thousand dollars in a big-jackpot game (it would have been more, but he had to share the prize with two others who had bingoed at the same time). When he got his money, he bought a truck from someone in the bingo-palace parking lot.

It's tempting to think that in the great bingo accounting of Uncle Vic's life, he's in the black, but I'm not so sure this is the case. He is lucky, there is no doubt about that. He has won at raffles, crib tournaments, lotteries, and just about every other game of chance. But we never heard about how much money he *spent* on his bingo habit over the years. One of the comforting things about the psychology of bingo is that you never actually *lose*. You just don't win sometimes.

I suspect Uncle Vic knew at some level that he was carrying on a family tradition with his bingo-playing, just as Aunt Blanche continued the family legacy in her devotion to the Church. He was very close to Grandma, perhaps because he was the youngest child of the family. When Grandma died at the age of ninety-one, he was one of the hardest hit. I remember sitting with him in his truck after Grandma's funeral in Vancouver—Glenn, Michelle, and I— trying to console him for a loss that he couldn't even measure or comprehend.

"I can't believe Mom's gone," he said, again and again. "I just can't believe it." We sat there, cramped in the cab of his truck, while the other cars filed out of the funeral-home parking lot. I had never seen him like this: at a loss for a joke, a nudge, a laugh. His face was utterly blank. But I could see that he was struggling with something, trying to find a way of expressing his grief. The last of the funeral cars was gone when he finally pulled his keys out of his pocket and inserted the ignition key with a flourish of decisiveness.

"What we should do," he said, "is we should go to a bingo. Mom would have wanted it that way."

He was only half joking. Less than half. We drove down the avenues of West Point Grey and Kerrisdale, looking for a bingo hall, reminiscing about Grandma's proclivities for any and all games of chance. But Uncle Vic's unerring bingo-palace homing instinct was not well tuned that afternoon. He was thrown off by the tide of gentrification that had swept across the city in recent years. After an hour of searching, we gave up and drove back to Aunt Blanche's place, where most of the other relatives had gathered.

We felt vaguely defeated, even though I hadn't been particularly thrilled with the prospect of sitting in a smoky room marking circles on a mysterious grid of paper. But all was not lost. We heard that Vic went out again later in the day, by himself, and he found a bingo-palace, where he was able to grieve in the most genuine and possibly the most satisfying manner. I like to think that he had borrowed Grandma's lucky 777 Bingo dabber for the occasion. I do know that when he got back to the hotel later that evening, there was a look of consolation on his face. And his pockets were jingling.

Grandma and Grandpa Strelau.

GRANDMA *and* GRANDPA

Learning about Grandma Laliberte made me think again about my grandparents on the other side of the family. Grandma and Grandpa Strelau had been gone for years already by this time, and they had become little more than static memories, flashes of shorthand recollection that came to me whenever I thought of them: Grandpa standing in the foliage of his garden, hunting for potato beetles; Grandma kneading dough at the kitchen counter, her flowery dress swaying with each knuckled punch. It was time to re-remember them. Not so much to find out their secrets, if they had any, but to consider how I had come from them, how I had been created in the shape of their lives. They were a part of me too; I had taken their place in the world. And yet I understood very little about where they had come from, what they had wanted from their lives, what they intended to pass down to later generations.

Grandma and Grandpa Strelau lived in Canwood, a town that got its name from the contraction of Canadian Wood. But I knew they weren't from there, not originally. Grandpa had come from Poland, even though he was

German rather than Polish, and perhaps his time in Poland was what had contributed to his vehement dislike of Catholics. He came to Canada at the age of nineteen with his brother Karl, and they took up homesteads between Canwood and the village of Ordale. Grandma and Grandpa met soon afterward. Like their homesteader neighbours, who were immigrants from various parts of Europe, they laboured for years to break the land, to build houses and barns, and to set in enough food and firewood to survive the winters.

Grandma's family were Norwegian but they had lived for a generation in Minnesota before making the trek northward to settle in the Canadian woods. She was born in the States and was three years old when they moved. I didn't realize this until long after her death. I would never in a million years have guessed that she was technically an American. She seemed purely Norwegian to me. She spoke with a strong accent, full of vowels and "y" sounds and lilting, off-centred syllabic emphasis. "*Uffda*" was her favourite expression of surprise or chagrin or delight. She had several brothers living in the Canwood area, all of them impossibly tall, skinny men. I remember Uncle Otto and Uncle Joe: both over six-foot-seven, both bachelor farmers and trappers.

Grandma herself was quiet, placid, yet always busy in the yard, the garden, the house. We loved to eat the *lefse* she made, the Norwegian flatbread that was something like a communion wafer but much larger and more tasty. She used to heat up the wood stove in the basement and bake sheets of *lefse* the size of the entire stovetop. They cooked in seconds, the thin sheet of dough browning in its distinctive freckled spots. And then she reached underneath with a long stick and flipped the whole sheet over for another few seconds. We devoured it hot when we had the chance, just as it was starting to get brittle in the stacks beside the stove. It looked like piles of stripped birchbark. She kept it, dried, in the back of the cupboard, and it stayed fresh there for months. We used to break off crumbs and crunch it into a mashed-potatoey pulp. For special occasions she softened it by storing it with a damp tea towel, and it became an entirely different food. We smeared butter on one side, then rolled it into tubes and devoured it, sometimes dipping it in turkey gravy or cranberry sauce.

Grandpa was a prodigious and single-minded berry picker. When Mom was growing up, picking berries had been not only a fun way of spending an afternoon but also a necessary source of food in a place where fruit was often unavailable. Grandpa was the master of volume berry picking, and even in later life when the berries were no longer required for their nutrients, he picked pails upon pails of blueberries, raspberries, saskatoons, and chokecherries. He had even made a blueberry-picking tool in their early years on the farm. It was a wide-toothed comb attached to a small bucket, and it worked very much like a bear's paw. The teeth of the comb raked through the plant and pulled off all the berries—ripe and green—along with many leaves, twigs, insects, and assorted detritus. Everything collected in the bucket, which Grandpa dumped periodically into larger pails or cardboard boxes. Then he brought them home, and Grandma canned them, made jellies and jams, made pies. She was an extraordinary canner. She filled hundreds of quart jars every summer, with every kind of produce from the garden and the wilds.

Grandpa also had a workshop in the basement where he fixed bicycles. He found old bikes in the dump or bought them at auctions or directly from his neighbours, and he took them home to clean them, paint them, change the bearings and the tires. I was fascinated with his storage shed beside the garden, where he had dozens and dozens of used bicycle parts: wheels, sprockets, and chains dangling from nails, tin chain guards and fenders piled against the wall, and at least twenty freshly painted frames hanging from the rafters. He would take one bike at a time down to his workshop and rebuild it, trying different spare parts, adjusting the spokes and brakes and chains. He had small boxes full of gleaming bearings the size of shotgun pellets.

These bikes were mostly old-fashioned ones, heavy steel, with wide saddle-like seats and upright handlebars. They had only single gears, and none had the radically curving handle-bars of the racing ten-speeds that were popular at the time. They were older than the banana bikes that were just becoming obsolete when I got into grade five. But still, there was a charm about these bikes, with their new brightly coloured skins, their solid-state construction, their wide and uncrashworthy metal fenders. When we could, we raced around town on them. Before that, there were two tricycles that Grandpa kept around for our use, and we would roll down the driveway, feet off the pedals, letting them spin like eggbeaters as we freewheeled toward the road.

Grandpa seemed most comfortable while working, either in his shop or in the garden, or sitting at the roll-top desk in his study, writing letters, with small round spectacles strapped onto his ears. He was not a storyteller like most of my Cariou relatives. He was a doer. When he was inside he often sat in his vinyl recliner and read his German Bible or his German newspaper. He could read and write English, but he always preferred German when possible, even though he rarely spoke it at home. Grandma had learned to speak it in the early years of their marriage, but I never heard her use the language. English was an uneasy bridge between them.

There was something about Grandma Strelau that I only gradually came to understand. Grandma, the *lefse* baker, fish scaler, berry canner, she of the gentle laugh, the *uffda,* the coy smile: she was sick. Diabetes, and then cancer. She never said anything to us about her illnesses, even when the cancer required major surgery and became severely debilitating. All I knew was that she had cancer, and that it was some kind of cancer that was embarrassing or difficult to talk about. I learned not to ask questions, not to think about Grandma's illness if at all possible, not to bring it up when talking with other people. We knew it had something to do with the nether regions, with sex or bowels or urination, but we also knew it would be awkward to ask.

Grandma's decline was not sudden, but still I was incredulous when we got the news that she had died. Mom had been to visit her the previous week but had returned home for a brief time. I don't remember Mom or Dad telling us that Grandma was not going to live, but maybe they did. In any case, I was shocked when Dad came out of the bedroom where he had been on the phone to Canwood and told us, "We're going to have to go to Canwood tomorrow to say goodbye to Grandma. She passed away this morning."

It was Mom's birthday. No one was supposed to cry on their birthday, but I could hear that she was, somewhere beyond the bedroom door. We had heard that sound a few times in the previous weeks, and now I understood why.

In the car the next morning, Mom cried again. She made no sound. The tears came out from the edges of her eyes, and she swept them away with the back of her hand. We didn't know what to say. I tried to look straight ahead, over Dad's shoulder. He looked at us in the rear-view mirror and kept telling us it wouldn't be long now until we got to Canwood, telling us to keep colouring our colouring books. But I was too old for colouring books. I gazed out the window, pretending I was riding a motorcycle in the ditch, jumping over road allowances and approaches. We drove east of town, through the St. Cyr Hills and past Green Lake, and then south into a different part of the Height of Land. Not far on the other side of it was Canwood.

By the time we arrived, Mom's tears were gone and I was queasy with the familiar carsick feeling. Many other vehicles were lined up around the corner in front of Grandma and Grandpa's house, and a gang of my cousins was wrestling on the front lawn.

"Hi, Auntie Melba! Hi, Uncle Ray!" they called, without interrupting their barrage of horseplay.

"Well if it ain't Carren Wariou," my cousin Randy said. "Betya can't do this!"

And he cartwheeled across the lawn, glancing off a knot of laughing, grunting Stampede Wrestler cousins. I knew I couldn't do it but I tried anyway, and my arms buckled, and my jaw snapped shut, and I lay there on my back trying to

laugh along with the rest of them while I ran my tongue over
my teeth to check for chips. Then someone pulled me
upright and I was running with the whole group of them
around the house, jumping over the downspouts, sliding in
the grass. Swarms of meteors arced in my field of vision. I
thought I might collapse or throw up, but in a few seconds I
was fine again and we were playing auntie-I-over, with one
group of us on each side of the house, punting a miniature
football over the living room and listening for the sound of it
landing. No one mentioned Grandma. I started to forget why
we were here.

When Uncle Art came out and yelled at us to stop
bouncing that goddamn football off the roof, Randy and I
snuck inside the house, past the visiting uncles and aunts in
the kitchen and down into the basement. We went for the
root-cellar door, with the beat-up dartboard hanging from it
and three plastic-finned darts imbedded in the panelling—
signs of a recent skirmish among the older cousins. I held the
door open for Randy so he would have some light to run in
and jump at the string that dangled from the bare light bulb.
He grabbed it on the third try, and we gazed up at the spindly
towers of homemade shelving units that surrounded us.

The room was a Babel of preserves: quart sealers stuffed
with parsnips, potatoes, turnips, boiled eggs, carrots, beans,
corn on the cob, rolled-up jackfish fillets, whole chickens
encased in sheaths of gelatinous goo, pickled onions, pickled
beets, mustard pickles, and three variations on the old-
fashioned cucumber dill. The room even smelled vaguely
briny, oceanic, from the decades of pickling that had occurred
there. But we weren't after the pickles, or the meat, or the

vegetables. Our quarry was stacked higher, along the topmost shelves, where the jar lids nearly touched the mossy beams of the ceiling. These jars were full of canned berries, which we called simply fruit: blueberry fruit, raspberry fruit, saskatoon fruit, rhubarb fruit. Berries suspended in thin sweet fluid, not too syrupy. We had always craved them, and had waited years for an opportunity like this.

Randy began to climb, pulling himself up to the third shelf, wedging a toe behind the thin wooden support rail. The whole shelf unit quivered, and the jars rang against each other with a sound like a telephone. I braced myself to catch him if he fell. He grunted and pulled himself in one swift chin-up onto the next shelf, then turned to grin at me.

"Hey," he said, nodding toward a jar of whole parsnips. "Peter Piper picked a peck a pickled peckers."

They were tumescent, vaguely hairy, startlingly pallid.

"Ya gotta watch out for old Peter," he laughed, dangling by one hand as he grabbed at his crotch with the other. Then he swung himself up to the next level so his feet were above my head.

"Jackpot!" he said.

We got two quart jars of saskatoons. I pried the rubber-ring lids open with an old nail I'd found on Grandpa's workbench. We sniffed at the fruit, each holding a jar by the neck as if to pour a pagan libation.

"Race ya," Randy said, and I heard his tooth ding against the glass as he shoved his face into the vast mouth of the jar. I leaned into my own jar and tasted the rich, sweet broth. A row of floating berries bounced against my upper lip, and then I opened my mouth wider and drank the berries too, without chewing, and their stems tickled in my throat. I inhaled a little between each swallow and then exhaled the same way, five mouthfuls to every breath. The sound echoed in the jar: *slup-hoot, slup-hoot, slup-hoot, slup-hooot*. I could hardly taste it anymore but the fluid was still silky on my tongue.

Through the mottled glass I saw Randy with his own jar tipped nearly upside down. He was going to win. But I swore to finish mine too, just to prove I could. I leaned my head back further and tried to relax my throat. A purple ocean was draining into me. Berries caromed off my uvula and spun down my esophagus. I could feel hundreds of them bobbing in my stomach like all the bottles ever tossed into the sea. I was dizzy, and the jar trembled in my hands, but still I kept up the rhythmic *slup-hoot, slup-hoot, slup-hoot*, and suddenly the liquid was gone. The last dozen berries trickled reluctantly down the glass and I munched on them queasily.

"Slowpoke," Randy said.

"Good to the last drop," I replied.

We hid the empty jars at the back of the parsnip shelf and then we staggered upstairs, afraid to look at each other, afraid even to belch, lest some accident should betray our secret. Randy went back outside, but I slipped into the living room and flopped down in Grandpa's recliner. *Gilligan's Island* was on.

Half an hour later Aunt Linda announced it was suppertime. She called Grandpa from his bedroom and he came out, squinting as if he didn't recognize us. His eyes seemed too small for their sockets, and the skin of his unshaven cheeks was almost blue. I didn't say hello to him. Aunt Linda helped him into the kitchen, and he sat at the table without speaking. He looked like he was trying to remember something—a word at the tip of his tongue, maybe a person's name, a phrase some-one had told him long ago. He was not usually a forgetful man.

I refused to eat the supper that Aunt Sharon brought on a TV tray. Even the tube of rolled-up *lefse* beside my mashed potatoes couldn't tempt me. The berries were still milling in my stomach. I watched my younger cousins stuff their pink faces with mounds of potatoes and turnips, pale slabs of roast beef. Out the window I saw Randy sitting on the hood of our car, holding the edge of his plate up to his mouth to catch a drizzle of dark gravy. I felt a rush of saliva under my tongue and sensed an oncoming tidal wave in the sea of bobbing berries, but I kept it down by breathing deeply, closing my eyes, rubbing my sweaty hands up and down on my pantlegs. When I felt well enough to open my eyes again, my *lefse* and my roast beef were gone, and several of my cousins were snickering. I thanked God for their treachery.

Mom and Aunt Linda came in to clear away the plates.

"And we have a very special dessert," Aunt Linda announced. "It's the last of Grandma's saskatoon fruit. So when you eat it, think of all the good things you remember about Grandma."

I was paralyzed, first with fear that they somehow knew about our theft, and then with a recognition of what we had really done. There would never be any more of that fruit. And we had wasted it.

Mom placed a crystal bowl full of berries on my TV tray. My stomach surged. Rabbit turds in an oil slick, with sugar sprinkled on top. The cousins were already eating blithely, secure in their ignorance of death. Their spoons chimed on the glass, and they sang, "Mmm mmm good!"

I deserved this.

I leaned forward in my chair, picked up my spoon, and lifted a purple mound to my lips. I ate gravely, slowly, each mouthful a taste of ashes.

When it was nearly bedtime, Mom and Dad called me into their bedroom, which was also Grandpa's study. We were the only ones left in the house besides him.

"How'd you like to help out your grandpa, Little Man?" Dad asked.

I didn't answer.

"Grandpa's feeling lonely and very tired," Mom said. "And we were thinking maybe you could sleep in his room tonight, just to keep him company. What do you think?"

If it hadn't been for the shame of the berries, I might have refused. But now I couldn't. I put on my pyjamas in Mom and Dad's room and then brushed my teeth, all the time asking myself why we had stolen those berries. I could never understand my motivations for sin.

Grandpa had always been a quiet man, a kind man. I had gone fishing with him many times, and we were great companions on the riverbank, chucking our lures into the water, laughing when either of us dragged up a clam instead of a fish. But I was afraid of him sometimes—afraid of his silence, his foreignness, his occasionally gruff demeanour. This evening he had seemed totally empty of feeling, of life.

Mom led me into the room. I had been there many times before, but never when it was dark outside. We used to go in there in the mornings, hoping to wake up Grandma and Grandpa, but they were always out of bed before we got there. We loved the feel of the crocheted lace bedspread, with its pattern of little cloth nubbins that made me think of a vast page of Braille. I knew the smell in there too, the slight rosiness of Grandma's perfume, the mustiness of antique furniture. On their dresser was the big German clock that clanged out the hour and the quarter hour so loudly it was audible throughout the house. Its black brass pendulum went *clack clack clack*, and somewhere inside, the mechanism whirred.

"That's your side," Mom whispered, and she pointed. It was Grandma's side. The coverlet was open, exposing a pale green sheet.

Mom waited for me to say my prayers, and then she tucked me in like she used to do after story time. There would be no stories tonight

"Come and get me if Grandpa needs anything," she said, and switched off the light. As the door closed behind her, the clock got louder. I turned onto my stomach and pulled the blankets over my head.

There was a shallow indentation in the mattress. From Grandma. For years and years she had lain in this spot, making a little hollow, like the nest of a deer. And now I was in it. Her place.

Was this the bed where she died?

I burrowed my head farther under the blankets, edged myself as far as possible out of the hollow. I had the idea that if I looked at the foot of the bed, Grandma would be standing there, her ghostly form giving off otherworldly light. The clock taunted me but I didn't look. I recycled my breath until I was hyperventilating, and then I opened a tiny snorkel hole for fresh air. Nothing could make me look.

The clock surprised me with a single clang. Quarter after nine. I lay there huddled at the edge of the indentation for two more soundings of the bell before Grandpa came in. Through my breathing hole I could see his shadow against the curtains. He closed the door without turning on the light, and then he stood there in the dark for a long time. I wondered again what he was thinking. Did he even know I was in here? Would he mistake me for Grandma?

There was a jingle of change in his pocket, and then the dead sound of clothes landing on carpet. The mattress rocked slightly, and I heard him whispering in German. Praying. Or maybe talking to Grandma.

The bed heaved sideways and I clung to the edge of the mattress as he rolled in. I breathed as loudly as I could, trying to feign the slow suck and wheeze of sleep, even though my heart was hammering. Would he want to talk to me about Grandma?

I listened. His breathing answered mine. Each exhalation was a sigh, almost a groan, as if the most basic business of living had become unendurable for him. I dreaded the accidental touch of his foot or his elbow. We lay there, breathing together. The clock told us to talk, talk, talk, but we said nothing. It counted out the stroke of ten, and banged again at ten-fifteen. Grandpa hadn't moved, but I could tell from the sound of his breath that he wasn't sleeping. Every so often he would hold the air in, as if to slip briefly under water.

It became a vigil: the two of us keeping watch on the night, pondering Grandma's place among the saints and our own places in the sorrowful world. I had never heard of a wake but I knew instinctively what we were doing. A night of alertness was the most fitting response to the long sleep of death. I devoted the time to remembering everything I could about Grandma: the smell of her hair, the feel of her generous hug, the dovelike sound of her voice. It was as if she was there with us after all, not as a ghost but as a denizen of memory.

I stayed awake past the long clanging of midnight, and then I slept. When I awoke, the room was full of sunlight and Grandpa was gone. I'd had a dream about him, which was really a memory from three or four years earlier. We had gone berry picking, just the two of us, along the banks of a muddy creek south of Canwood. On one bank was a grove of immense saskatoon bushes, twice as tall as Grandpa—they weren't shrubs, they were trees. The berries hung down in fist-sized clusters, silhouetted against the acetylene sky.

I clambered out and asked for my pail, but Grandpa hesitated. He looked at me, then at the dangling berries, then back at me.

"I think we don't pick to keep today," he said.

We walked to the base of the trees and I saw that he was right: they were too tall for me. I jumped once and snagged a single berry but crushed it in my fingers.

"Here," he said, and he scooped me up by the armpits, hoisted me into the sky. I felt the sun on my face, smelled the silty breath of the river, and gazed at the swollen berries that fed on both of them. I pulled a branch down to my mouth, closed my lips around a cluster of berries, and chewed them, still attached to the tree.

Grandpa began to laugh. My whole body quivered in the air.

IV

❧

Homing

What I love about the north: the fusion of land and liquid and sky.

HEART'S TERRITORY

Not long after my discoveries about my family's past, there was another change in my life: I met the woman who would become my partner, Alison. *Met* is not quite the right word, however. It was not the blithely fortuitous accident that my own parents' meeting had been, thirty years before. In fact it was a fix, carefully engineered by a group of our mutual friends back in Saskatchewan, though neither of us lived there anymore.

"Warren, there's a person you really should meet," they told me when I was back home the previous summer.

"She's a poet, a very fine—"

"Red hair—"

"And her laugh, it's like—"

"And a Saskatchewan gal, too. . . ."

They were somewhat less subtle with Alison.

"It's not that we want you to go out with Warren; it's just that we don't want you to ruin your life."

"Here's a picture of him to keep by your place at the table."

"If you carry this frozen brook trout back to Ontario on

the plane, Warren could come out to the airport and get it from you, and then you'd *meet*!"

When we finally did meet, seventeen months after the salvoes of hints and suggestions had begun, we were fully prepared to despise each other. It was at a Christmas party in Saskatoon, a party that may well have been arranged with the two of us in mind. We were not entirely cooperative, however. I arrived with a friend who was seven months pregnant. Alison refused to wear the elaborate ball gown that certain well-meaning friends had insisted on. We circled the room, staying at opposite ends, until our gracious host took the initiative and introduced us.

"I feel like I've known you all my life," she said. It didn't sound like a compliment.

But the conspiracy at least gave us something to discuss. We whispered about them, plotting counter-insurgency, non-compliance, mutiny. We wondered what we had done to deserve such treatment. And somehow by the end of the evening we were thinking of ourselves as something like a team.

"You're not half as bad as I'd been led to believe," she admitted.

"You neither."

Love.

We courted by stories—told over e-mail and telephone at first, and then during weekend visits between my place in Toronto and hers in London, Ontario. I regaled her with the misadventures of my multitudinous relatives, and with some of Dad's rambling anecdotes about Meadow Lake and Ituna, and with much of the quirky folklore of the north. She had fewer relatives to choose from, but she matched my stories with her own, building a composite picture of her life that included her birth in England, a smart-alecky childhood in Saskatoon, a maniacal (and inherited) devotion to the Saskatchewan Roughriders, and a fondness for gophers.

Sometimes we stopped laughing. I told her about Clayton, about Marie Clemence, about Dad's heart attack and my growing sense of disconnection from my home. She told me about her parents' divorce, her grandmother's recent illness and death. Her father had had a heart attack too. We wondered about our futures: where we would end up, what we would be doing in four or five years.

Before long we decided to move in together, so we signed a lease on an apartment in London and we made our plans. One afternoon a few weeks later I found myself driving a rented van down the busiest highway in Canada, with my boxloads of clothes and books and plants and stereo equipment piled up in the back, trying to follow Alison's brown Toyota through the seething capillaries of southern Ontario traffic. On the move again. I felt few regrets, even though I had enjoyed Toronto. In fact, by this time moving seemed almost normal. It was staying still that felt unnatural. I could sense that all around the globe at that moment, as I careened down the rush-hour 401 in pursuit of a rusting old Camry, more people than ever before were moving—by car and jetliner and dinghy and helicopter and camel—all of them consumed with the thought of their destinations and the destinations after that. It was okay. You could get accustomed to this speed, to this trail of other drivers zooming along beside you and behind you and in front of you. You could follow that other car to wherever the hell it was going and wherever it went after that. After a while, it would start to feel like the two of you were stationary and the earth was rotating beneath you.

Only a few weeks later we were travelling again, heading for home. It was time to meet each other's families, to show each other our former stomping grounds. So we loaded our tent and our luggage in the old brown car and drove west.

"If you show me your Saskatchewan," I said, "I'll show you mine."

Neither of us knew what we were in for.

We had thought of Saskatchewan as something we had in common, but in fact we'd had very different upbringings. For one thing, she was from the south, and from a city. She thought 4-H and curling were somehow funny. She had never walked on muskeg. For my part, I couldn't understand the concept of childhood in suburbia.

"So from the ages of ten to sixteen, you basically lived in the mall. . . ."

"At least I didn't live on the set of *Deliverance*."

"Haw haw."

"Puddle *ding* ding *ding* ding *ding* ding *ding* . . ."

We each had much to learn. When we arrived in Saskatchewan she gave me the tour of her Saskatoon life, showing me her grandmother's house on Elliott Street, where her name was written in the concrete sidewalk, and taking me out to her favourite Dairy Queen on Eighth Street, where a hot fudge sundae brought back a flood of reminiscences. She had grown up in the flight path of the Saskatoon International Airport, a mere four blocks from the Mall at Lawson Heights. She couldn't tell oats from barley, Holsteins from Herefords, Barred Rocks from Rhode Island Reds. And yet she was a prairie girl in some way that I couldn't quite fathom.

And it turned out that she knew something about the north. I was vaguely disconcerted to learn that she had actually inhabited the parkland for brief but memorable times in her childhood. Her family had owned a cabin at Loon Lake, no more than an hour's drive from Meadow Lake, and they had spent weeks there every summer. If she had still been going there in the eighties, I might have seen her on the beach at the Little Jumbo resort, or in the cluttered aisles of the Dew Drop Inn general store on the highway, where we often stopped to buy sunflower seeds on the way to Uncle Hank's new cabin at Murphy Lake. But their family cabin was sold in 1979 just after Alison's parents were divorced, and she had never seen it again. One of our purposes in this journey was to go back there and see what remained of the place.

She told me about the cabin on the way there: it was a real log cabin like the homesteaders used to make, except it was painted green and had a porch that looked out toward the beach. She had learned to read there, she said, and she even remembered the names of her first two books: *This Is the Zoo* and *This Is the Farm*. And every time they drove the boat past a particular overhanging pine tree, they would gaze up into the branches to see Uncle Ernie's long-lost silver jackfish plug, which had swayed there in the breeze for years. She remembered that the lake was a wide, perfect circle, with a shock of a treed island on the far side, and powdery white beaches flecked with bits of charcoal and twigs and sunflower seeds and tiny swirling seashells. At one time their cabin was the only one on this side of the lake.

But everything had changed. When we stepped out onto the beach, we saw dozens of docks jutting out toward the middle of the lake like the spokes of a hubless wheel, and boats were everywhere: boats dangling in the air from spindly hoists, boats tethered to buoys, boats hauled halfway up on the shore. The beach too was littered with watercraft: Jet Skis, canoes, sailboards, catamarans, kayaks, pedal-boats, flutterboards, rowboats. There was hardly a place to sit down. And despite the plethora of brightly coloured equipment, there was no one on the entire beach except us.

I knew the cabin would be gone, and I think Alison knew too. But still we walked up and down the beach, stepping over anchor ropes and boardwalks and dormant machinery, gazing at the cabin fronts. After a while we became accustomed to the eerie vacancy of the place and started to enjoy ourselves. We skipped stones on the calm water and waded out among the boats to catch hair-thin water snakes, which we tied in loose knots so we could watch them untie themselves and swim away. Later in the afternoon we would fish for perch from the ends of the multitudinous piers, using handlines and tiny hooks baited with beef jerky bought from the store.

But first we had to find the cabin, or the place where the cabin had been.

"I think it was here," Alison said, looking in at a tidy little A-frame with three blue Jet Skis dragged up on the beach. We had walked past it twice before. "I remember that pine tree, and the neighbour's cabin."

"You sure?"

She hesitated. I could see the furious concentration on her face, the torsion of memory working in her.

"No," she said. "I can't be sure."

And she stood there on the cluttered beach and cried.

After that it was my turn. We drove onward to Meadow Lake and stayed there for more than a week. My family was very welcoming, and just quirky enough to make some of my earlier stories seem plausible. The day after we arrived, Dad took us out to the pasture and called to the cattle with his plaintive and birdlike cry—"Come boss, come boss!"—just like I had said he would. Mom walked us through the garden, stopping to scold the weeds and to yank at them disgustedly. Uncle Vic dropped by and told us dirty jokes while whipping us at Rummoli. Aunt Marcia embraced Alison like a long-lost daughter. Mr. Lajeunesse called her Skinny Little Red-Haired Girl. We sat in the backyard swatting mosquitoes while Dad grilled steaks ("from our own beast," he said several times), and Glenn and Michelle told her many false-hoods about my supposed childhood cruelties and teenage inanities. After supper we walked the whole perimeter of the farmyard, and then sat up in the hayloft and watched the sun setting behind the granaries, over the radiant barley field.

"Most beautiful place in the world," I said, and she didn't disagree.

After a couple of days on the farm, we rambled around the district. First we made a haphazard pilgrimage along the sandy trails of Leonard's Ranch, watching for cattle and mushrooms and arrowheads, and then we went to the cabin at Jeannette Lake for a day of windsurfing, swimming, fishing, and tentative muskeg-walking. One afternoon we drove out to Steele Narrows, where we picked dusty chokecherries from the roadside bushes and then brought them home and made a clotted, half-congealed jelly that looked like the leavings of a slaughterhouse.

"*Tastes* perfectly good," Mom said encouragingly.

I took Alison out to the Bielby place, a homestead where I had worked for part of a summer when I was in university. It had been the home of Mrs. Verley Bielby for more than forty years, and after she died I had been hired by Mrs. Bielby's daughter to restore part of the property, which had been designated a provincial heritage site. As Alison and I wandered in the yard, past lilacs and rhubarb and the reassuringly solid presence of the cabin, I told her about my time there. I had "mudded" the holes between the logs in that cabin, mixing together clay and sand and straw in an old galvanized bathtub, and then pressing it into the empty spaces with my bare hands. I had even lived out there for a while, becoming almost a homesteader myself. In the evenings I sat on an ancient homemade rocking chair in the cabin, sometimes reading and sometimes just imagining the lives that had been lived there. And I began to feel a real kinship with Verley Bielby, though I had never met her. I pieced together a life for her, from the photos on the walls, the furniture, and the stories I had heard from Mom and Dad and the neighbours. And I got a better sense of her from the place itself: its meticulous orderliness, even three years after her death; the smoothness of the arms on that rocking chair that had been polished by the daily presence of hands. She had imprinted the place with her life.

"Sounds like quite a lady," Alison said. "Sounds like your grandma."

Yes. Maybe that was why I felt at home in this old farmyard: because it was the likeness of a place I had heard about all my life, the farm at Ituna where Dad had been raised.

The next day we drove north past Beauval in search of blueberries. They were scarce that year, but they seemed to grow best near the roadside shrines, where small white crosses and large statues of the Virgin Mary served as memorials to the road's many accident victims. On the way home we stopped at Fraser's Museum, an extensive and disparate collection of northern Saskatchewan artifacts, from old outboard motors to Cree Bibles to bone scrapers and arrowheads, presided over by a Cree septuagenarian named John Fraser, who had been collecting museum bric-a-brac since he was eight years old.

"I told my mom," he said, "I told her I was gonna keep my lunch pail—that red lard pail right there on the second shelf—and I was gonna put it in a museum of my own someday. Oooh, did she laugh! But I did it, I built this museum with my own hands. And them pails, they're worth big money now."

Fraser himself was the most fascinating exhibit in the place: a huckster historian, an inveterate teaser, a storyteller extraordinaire. As we were leaving he tried to sell us his piano, his homemade gazebo, and his three-legged dog. We settled for a pair of elk-antler earrings made by his wife.

As we drove back home through the Flying Dust reserve, with the calm waters of Meadow Lake shining in the distance and the comforting blue ribbon of the Height of Land enclosing the whole southern vista, I glanced over at her.

"So?" I said.

"So what?"

"Well . . . what do you think of it all?"

I needed some judgment from her, some appraisal of my place—though I suppose it was as much a test of her as of Meadow Lake. She must have sensed this, because she didn't answer for a long time. She gazed out toward the western horizon, where the grain elevators of town were just coming into view.

"Well, I can see why you are how you are," she said finally.

"And how's that?"

"No comment."

We drove past the old stockyards and the abandoned creamery, and then into town, past the trailer park, car wash, Hannigan's Hamburger Shack, RCMP station, Happy Inn, liquor store. Hardly an idyllic picture. I saw it all as she would, and was embarrassed by my enthusiasms.

"It's not home to me," she said. "But still. I love the way you love this place."

I supposed that was all anyone could hope for.

Alison on the way to Mamquam.

MAMQUAM LAKES

In our life away from Meadow Lake, Alison and I continued our travels, wandering with our car and our camping gear in Southern Ontario, Michigan, New York State, Maine, Cape Breton Island. Even though we didn't think of the East as home, we wanted to understand the place by rambling through it. Then, in the summer of 1998, we moved to Vancouver, where I had been offered a teaching job at UBC, and before classes began we decided to learn about our new place by hiking in the surrounding mountains. We had seen plenty of mountains as visitors to the region, but neither of us had ever felt that we had *inhabited* them, even briefly. It seemed to me that if we were going to stake any kind of claim to belonging here, even in the most tentative sense, then we would have to camp out and make our own temporary home, to subsist there in the coastal wilderness with all its dangers and wonders and unknowns. We were not wanting exactly to put down roots—the place was too strange, too exotic, for that—but at least to make a campsite, a place that would be ours for a couple of nights.

We had already made the trek up to Garibaldi Lake for our first overnight camping trip, where we had camped among clumps of fragrant heather and had looked out at the mirror reflection of the glacier on the lake. I had cast in the frigid, gin-clear water for gorgeous rainbow trout, and had caught several of them in front of an audience of snowboarders, who had declared me "sick!" as they hoisted their boards up on their shoulders and began their search for snow. Garibaldi had been a wonderful start, but now—before the brief summer at altitude was over—we wanted to take on one more challenge: to hike into a wilderness, with no campground, no park ranger, no fellow campers with hauled-in ghetto blasters pouring Limp Bizkit across the heather. We wanted to feel that we were entirely on our own, away from the world altogether.

That was what camping had meant for me in Meadow Lake—an escape. There were campgrounds, but we never went to them. We camped instead in the bush. I remember camping out at Leonard's Ranch once, when Glenn and I were very young and Michelle was still a baby. We were across the river, near the best fishing spot. It was just after the new bridge had been built. I remember the sound of the coyotes echoing in the river valley. It frightened me a little but mostly it made me wonder what the coyotes were saying. I loved the smell of the canvas tent, the flappy, walloping sounds it made when anyone moved, and the way the orange canvas glowed like a Halloween pumpkin when the morning sunlight touched it.

We were always camping "off somewhere," on the bank of a river or a lake, where there was no official campground, though often there were marks of sites where other people had made firepits. This was real camping: getting out of the grids and paths and patterns that marked our existence in towns and cities. We would bring our own water along, and burn our garbage in the firepit, and shit in the woods, balanced over the makeshift commode of a felled tree. Dad took great pains to ensure that we left everything as we had found it, and he was of course particularly fastidious about putting out the fire. We used to pee on the firepit afterward, "just to make sure."

Whenever I went camping in later life, it was like re-enacting those early excursions. Even when I explored a place very different from Meadow Lake, there was a sense that I felt at home with the activity, the being-outdoors, so that camping was a way of feeling closer to home, even when I wasn't geographically close to it at all.

In Meadow Lake it was—and still is—possible to drive to a beautiful place in the woods and to have it pretty much all to yourself. In Vancouver, at least within a few hours' drive, that is virtually impossible. To find seclusion in southern British Columbia, you have to hike. And so we decided to outfit ourselves for the backcountry and find the most secluded spot we could. I also had an additional requirement: I wanted to fish for the high mountain cutthroat and rainbow trout that B.C. is famous for. After poring over our collection of new hiking books and fishing books, I found the ideal route: the hike to the Mamquam Lakes, two days into the Garibaldi range. It would take us past mountain ridges, glaciers, an extinct volcano, and tiny jewel-like lakes. The final destination was a hidden valley that cradled the glacial Mamquam Lakes—the habitat of some of the province's most beautiful and plentiful trout. It was a wilderness campsite, and few people ever hiked there because it was so far from the trailhead.

We packed up our hiking gear and left early on Thursday morning, stopping for breakfast at the McDonald's in Squamish for a last greasy taste of civilization. We had phoned our families, left descriptions of what we were wearing and where we were going, and we felt confident that we were ready. It was unnerving to be going out beyond the reach of telephones, but the prospect was also enormously inviting, especially since I would be starting a new teaching job in less than three weeks. For this short time we could set aside all the stresses of moving and settling into new jobs. In addition to these worries, it turned out that Dad was in the hospital in Saskatoon for tests. He had been feeling tired and hadn't been sleeping well. But I'd phoned him the morning we left and he was feeling well enough to talk about more than the weather. He had golfed several times in the previous few days and he was determined to be ready for the tournament the following weekend, when three of his brothers were coming to play.

We drove the dusty, potholed logging road up to the trailhead, pulled on our boots, and hoisted our heavier-than-ever packs. There were many cars in the parking lot, but we had been assured that the vast majority of the people would be going to Elfin Lakes, the halfway point of our journey. We would stop there overnight on the way in, but then we would have Mamquam to ourselves for two nights.

We climbed through an unimaginably tall conifer forest for a long time, moving slowly against the steep grade, trying to learn the trick of balancing the pack, adjusting the multitudinous stays and buckles and straps, heaving and shifting ourselves up what the guidebook said was the longest of the hills. We met numerous hikers, most with daypacks or even less—some in running shoes with no protection from the treacherous rocks. It was difficult hiking, but we were smitten with the place already: the shade of the colossal trees, the huge broad leaves of the groundcover plants, the mysterious glowing berries along the path. We didn't dare to eat them but we imagined what each of them would taste like: the orange ones bitter, the black ones tart, the red ones bursting with syrupy sweetness.

We didn't talk much. We took turns walking in front so we would each have the chance of an unimpeded view. By midmorning we had reached a plateau, a broad plain of grass and shrubs and occasional spruce trees. To the east were the jagged spear points of the Tantalus Range, perpetually snow-covered, the most violent and barbaric-seeming of all the mountains on the coast. They seemed very close, though we knew they were miles away, across Howe Sound. I suppose that's how they got their name.

It was extraordinarily hot considering the altitude. The trail was dusty, powdery, and the fine particles clung to the sweat on our legs, forming drizzles and spots. We stirred our way onward, squinting at the northern horizon with its jumble of peaks superimposed on each other. Somewhere up there was the Garibaldi glacier, where we had been a few weeks earlier. We might get a view of it again on our second day of hiking.

In the meadows we saw clusters of a more familiar berry: blueberries. But the plants were tall—up to my knees—and the berries were the size of marbles. "Tame berries" we used to call these when we saw them in the supermarket back in

Saskatchewan. We had always scorned them, considering them markedly inferior to our wild blueberries. I thought of them in fact as a different food altogether, not of the angelic order of the blueberry. I voiced my disdain for these bloated berries to Alison, and I didn't even bother to eat any for at least half an hour, even though they were dangling over the path like grapes in a vineyard.

But when I did pluck off a dusty berry and eat it, I was amazed.

"These are *good!* Almost like the real thing!"

And I grabbed some more, greedily, and sucked them one at a time out of my open palm, Grandma Laliberte–style, like bingo balls exiting the machine. It was manifestly unfair that the coast should have mammoth blueberries and virtually no mosquitoes and not much winter to speak of.

They were everywhere: shrubs full of blueberries for miles, up and down the plateau, so that when I looked far away, the hills had a slight Wedgwood blue tinge to them. It was my childhood fantasy come true: more berries than anyone could possibly eat. I was irked that we had to keep hiking. I wanted nothing more than to lie down in the grass, like Grandma, and eat until I was stuffed.

Unfortunately, some other creatures had the same idea, and they were acting on it. It is a truth universally acknowledged that where there are blueberries there are bears. This place was no exception. Black bears dotted the landscape like cattle in a pastoral painting. They grazed leisurely on the berries, munching contemplatively, not taking the slightest notice of the brightly clad hikers who stood in clusters and pointed, and finally moved warily on.

The bears looked so harmless—so *vegetarian*—that it was difficult to muster any fear in this situation, but I knew that the lack of fear could also be dangerous around wild animals. Some of the other hikers were venturing a little closer than they should. Alison had never seen bears out in the open before, and she alternated between paralysis and an unhealthy desire to go closer, to examine these creatures as a *Wild Kingdom* camera might.

I had done that as a kid in Meadow Lake, along with the rest of the family, but we had done it from the safety of the car. We used to drive from our cabin to the garbage dump near Flotten Lake (we called it the Flotten Bear Amphitheatre) to watch the bears come out at dusk and root through the leavings of human civilization. They stuck their heads into empty tin cans, ripped open garbage bags, chewed and licked and pawed their way through the foulest, rottenest heaps of garbage. Around them, wisps of smoke sometimes came up: residual combustion from the fires that were set there once a week. With the smoke and the clouds of ash that rose from under their feet, not to mention the ungodly fishy, intestinal odours of the garbage dump, it seemed to me that this was ursine hell. Degraded, made a spectacle before their fellow mammals, the beasts did in fact appear vaguely ashamed of themselves for their addiction to garbage. And we were fascinated by them. We watched their territorial standoffs over particular mounds of refuse. We rolled the windows down a crack, wiggled our fingers outside. Sometimes the bears came to inspect the cars, not out of belligerence but reciprocal curiosity. We rolled up the windows in a frenzy, yelled for Dad to start the car, and cringed away from the brownish, quivering muzzles. They sniffed at us with an air of uncertainty, almost distaste, before returning to the stinking, smouldering smorgasbord that we and our kind had laid out for them.

Bears had always loomed large in my childhood imagination. When we were kids, Mom and Dad used to give us pots and pans to bang on as we walked through the woods. We were trusted to behave sensibly around bears, to keep our distance and continue making noise. "They're more scared than you are," Dad told us, but I found that hard to believe. I had heard the stories about the movie *Grizzly*—a landlocked version of *Jaws*—and I sometimes imagined meeting a rogue bear, one with a taste for human flesh.

In Meadow Lake there was always the possibility that we would encounter a bear, no matter where we were. Shortly after we moved to the farm, Mom came back to the house from the raspberry patch one afternoon and looked back to see a black bear standing among the raspberry canes, scooping berries into his mouth. Dad got his rifle and shot it, right there in the garden. I don't know why. He would never have done that up at the lake. I suppose it was what farmers were expected to do, to protect their farms. The bear he shot eventually became a bearskin rug, complete with ferocious plastic fangs and a livid fake tongue. At Mom's insistence, we kept it downstairs. We used to trip on its outstretched claws when we were bringing food up from the freezer.

Dad had shot quite a few animals over the years at the farm. All the farmers did it. Skunks, weasels, rats, coyotes, foxes—all were fair game because of what they would inevitably do to the chickens. Magpies were shot because they were thought to be filthy birds that ate robins' eggs. But Dad's methods were unorthodox. He shot a skunk once in our garage. Yes, *in* it. The garage was unusable for months. At the same time, he managed to shoot his car, the garage door, and the lawn mower, all of which were sprayed with ricocheting pellets from the single shotgun blast.

These coastal blueberry-fed bears were far more dignified than the Dumpster-diver bears we used to watch, but it was easy to see that they could become addicted to human food too, if the opportunity arose. At almost every rest stop on the trail, chipmunks appeared out of nowhere and began to beg. At Garibaldi Lake, our food supplies had been plundered by chipmunks, which had chewed right through our nylon packs to get their dinner. The more people gawked at these bears and tried to disturb them, the more they would become accustomed to human company, and that would be when the danger might really arise.

We continued past the herds of grazing bears, walking determinedly in the hot sun, watching the panorama extend on our left as we came into a fuller view of another unnamed range, with its ridges of black, twisted peaks and the languid blankets of glacier-snow smattered near the tops. The trail became rockier, less dusty, and we clomped along as if walking on broken chunks of cement. We followed a long ridge, which was exposed to a cool breeze with a tinge of the glaciers still on it, and this refreshed us a little. Eventually we dropped down into a slight valley on the far side of the ridge and spotted the ranger station, the campground, and the gorgeous blue pools of the tiny Elfin Lakes. To the north, across a wide valley, was a line of Garibaldi peaks, several of them encrusted with gleaming, amethystine glaciers. Their snowpack had melted away, leaving slick, reflective, bluish patches of ice that looked like raw gemstones: aquamarine or emerald or turquoise. Now we saw where the colour of glacial lakes came from.

But when we stopped at the Ranger station, we learned that the campground was closed. A mother bear and her two cubs had taken a particular liking to the blueberries near the camp, and the park ranger had decided it was too dangerous to allow the hikers in there. We asked her if she thought we should just push on and camp in the wilderness farther along the trail. But she said there was no water for a long distance after Horsetail Creek, and after that the landscape was mostly volcanic ash for quite a distance. She said we could camp near the ranger station instead, which was great because it had the most glorious view in the whole area.

We set up our tent with the door facing northward, so the last thing we would see that night, and the first thing the next morning, was the magnificent range to the north. That was where we would be hiking the next day—right up to the edge of those glaciers and then down to another valley where the Mamquam Lakes were. We sat in the tent to try out the view, and then we explored our surroundings for the rest of the afternoon, eating berries and watching out for bears and fellow hikers. We waded in the cool water of one of the lakes, soaking our blisters, rinsing the dust off our calves. And then we went back to the campsite and just sat there on the ground, grinning, trying to absorb the magnificence of what we'd discovered. We were giddy with altitude and fatigue. We made supper and ate it in silence, gazing out at the mountains we would be in tomorrow. As the sun went down, the glaciers, along with the sky, glowed like reawakened embers.

When night came, we sat in the tent with the flap open, still watching the shadows of the northern range, the luminescence of those immense upturned pieces of the world, silhouetted against the lingering twilight.

This twilight, it seemed, was moving. And almost growing brighter. Then we realized what it was: northern lights. Even this far south! They were distant, almost miniaturized, but undeniably aurora. Tongues of light curled out above the peaks, dropped their tendrils down toward the glaciers, faded away. I told Alison about the northern lights I had seen at Jeannette Lake, reflecting in the utterly calm water after our midnight bonfires, and I told her about Dad's belief that we could call to them, make them dance. These ones looked too far away to hear our whistling, so we sat quietly and watched them oscillate against the bulk of the mountains. After a while, we climbed into our sleeping bags and fell asleep with the outer flap of the tent still open, the light still moving in the north.

NIGHT

That was the night my dad died. His heart was weaker than the doctors had known. A hole opened up in the side of it, and all the technology in the world couldn't save him. Mom was with him when he died, but the rest of us were away: Glenn was back in Meadow Lake, Michelle and her husband, Bob, were in Calgary, and Alison and I were in the middle of nowhere. Mom didn't even know where we had gone.

Sunrise at Elfin Lakes, on the way to Mamquam.

CINDERS

We woke up early to the gleam of sunrise against the glaciers, the grey stonework of the mountains, the bristling green of distant spruce trees. We crawled out of our sleeping bags, put on water to boil for tea, and I retrieved our food from the chalet where most of the other hikers were sleeping. We wanted an early start, before the sun got too hot. By late afternoon I would be casting to rising trout along the shores of Mamquam Lake. We would have two days of solitude there, of freedom. We were both eager to get moving, so we hurried through our cereal, our tea, our granola bars. The sun was warm already. It cast brilliant light on the shambles of a mountain to the west of us, which had seemed nondescript in the evening. Now it was a crumbling fortress, decorated at its base with eons of its own tailings. A few pine trees clung to the cracks in the rock, one of them hanging there upside down. I could smell the dew, and the coming heat and dust and sweat. We took down the tent, rearranged our packs, and began our hike into the heart of the wilderness.

There was another blueberry meadow, inhabited by the bear cubs and their mother. We stopped to watch them for a minute, and then set off around the trail to give them extra space. I ate handfuls of blueberries as we moved through the meadow, hoping they would be even bigger and more succulent at Mamquam. There would be bears there too, I supposed, but I didn't want to think about that.

After the meadow, we hiked a long downhill into the valley on a narrow, shifting path. I went first, wondering about bears and knowing this trail was not as well travelled as the previous day's path. We sang, to keep the bears away. "Go Tell It on the Mountain." "Seven Bridges Road." "*Doot da doot da doot. Pa tum pa tum pa tum.*" "Yes, we have no blue-bear-ies, we have no blueberries today. . . ." It seemed that we were completely alone already, that we were free to be goofy when we wanted, free to talk to the bears, the mountains, the trout waiting for us in the lakes.

We descended farther, and the trail became wide enough for only two boots side by side. On the left were high banks, tree roots, a soil made of grey volcanic ash; on the right a steep drop of sometimes twenty feet, sometimes eighty. The trees grew well in this powdery soil, but the ground was shifty, unstable for walking. I leaned on my fishing rod tube (which I had learned to use as a walking stick) and tried to persuade Alison to carry a stick too, but she refused.

With a heavy pack it's harder to go downhill than up. We stopped several times on the way down. Eventually the creek came into view below: a roaring, boulder-strewn stretch of unending rapids. On the far side was a lunar desolation of volcanic ash and bleached stones. Farther north was the steep rampart of the Cinder Cone, the source of the apocalypse of ash that had blanketed the area generations ago. There was another group of hikers at the river, either stopping for a rest or trying to decide how to get across the raging water.

It was hotter in the valley floor, despite the breeze off the glacial river water. We slogged on, picking our way through boulders at the edge of the river, and stopped once to refill our water bottles. The beauty was different down here: stark, brilliant in the noonday light, almost dizzying with radiant heat. It reminded me of the Badlands in southern Alberta, the *mauvaise terre* where the prairie fell away into a variegated pit of ash and columnar hoodoos that every year, in the rain and wind, disgorged the skeletons of mythic beasts.

We passed the other hikers at the river crossing, which was not so treacherous as it had looked from a distance. They were just having lunch there, it turned out. We boulder-hopped without even getting our feet wet, and kept going across the flattest part of the ash field, where the sun seemed to radiate out of the ground. Dust rose with our footsteps; a grittier dust than we had walked through before, and our boots left perfect footprints in it, like astronauts on the Moon. There was no vegetation at all; only rock and dust and more rock. It was only half a mile through the ash field before we would cross another, smaller stream and then climb the rampart to stare down into the bowl of the cinder cone, where the earth had blown a hole in itself not so long ago. We would have our lunch there, and then push on to the ridge above the lakes.

What stopped us was an unnatural sound. A shriek, from somewhere behind us. It wasn't a marmot or a pika or a bird.

We scanned behind us and saw the hikers still back at the river. The sound again. Shrill—a whistle, a referee's whistle. Or a bear whistle. Something totally out of place in that barren land. We saw someone coming toward us, a small person stepping quickly, holding an open hand up in the air. It was the park ranger. I could see her hat and the long red ponytail bobbing behind it.

"I bet the campground is closed," Alison said. "Too many bears."

The ranger reached us in a couple of minutes, scrambling over the rocks without looking down. I felt no alarm at all; only disappointment that we might not be able to see the lakes.

"You Warren and Alison?" she said when she got within a dozen paces. At the sound of my name in the mouth of this stranger, I was suddenly stricken. There was something about her face, a tightness in her shoulders.

"Yes," I said.

"You have to come back to the ranger station. I got a message this morning that the RCMP are looking for you. They didn't say what it is, but they gave a number for you to phone. You can use the radio phone from the station."

She had been hiking for probably two hours, thinking about how she would say those words, and now she had said them and for a second she didn't know what else to do. Neither did we. A sound came from Alison, behind me, and I felt her hand on my shoulder, and my arm was around her waist, our packs banging together. We asked the ranger something (I can't remember what) and she said she didn't know, and then she said, "I'm going to go on ahead, I'll see you back at the station."

And then we were walking—knowing but not knowing, not quite daring to think about all the possibilities. We stepped in our own clean footprints, holding hands, nearly tripping sometimes but not stopping, not turning back even once to look at the shape of the Cinder Cone behind us. At the shriek of a whistle our lives had been reversed; we were not going to Mamquam Lake, we were going home. No matter what exactly had happened, we knew we would be home in a matter of hours. I have never felt so out of place as I did in those first few moments after the ranger spoke to us. As we stumbled back toward the clutch of hikers at Horsetail Creek, I was asking myself, What the hell am I doing here? How did I get to a place like this?

As we went farther I began to think more about home, about what had happened. I knew it was Dad, because of the tests, the fact that he had gone to the hospital, that he had been having trouble breathing the last few months. But was it too late, or was there still time for us to see him? Why the hell had we chosen this time to come out here, to escape from the world? There is no escape from the world, no matter where you live or where you go.

What if it wasn't Dad? What if it was one of Alison's parents, or Mom, or someone else in the family? The not knowing was like a magnification of the disaster, each of our loved ones suffering various fates in our minds. We kept walking, for more than two hours, up the same winding path of ash, across the river where the hikers looked inquisitively at us, and up the narrow valleyside trail. We took no breaks, we didn't look around us, we didn't think about what we were doing. We plodded like beasts. The nimble ranger soon disappeared in front of us, and we tried to talk about what might have happened, but all I could say was, "I know it's Dad," and all Alison could respond with was, "We *don't* know. We don't know anything."

And so we came out of the wilderness before we had really gone in, and we returned to a world that was utterly changed.

By the next afternoon we were driving north toward Meadow Lake, in a car borrowed from Alison's dad in Saskatoon. Mom and Glenn and Michelle were already back in Meadow Lake. We would be the last to arrive.

We travelled the intimately familiar route, over the North Saskatchewan, past the Battle River valley, through North Battleford, then the hills north of Cochin. The weather was hot and dry, the sun as painfully bright as it had been in the mountains, and everywhere the farmers were on the fields, their combines spewing trails of chaff into the air. The wheat was late-August bronze, even as it lay in the cut furrows waiting for the combine. We passed the familiar farmhouses, the blackened, abandoned buildings, the empty, sway-backed barn near Midnight Lake. They were no longer just signposts on a journey, beads on a string between the world and Meadow Lake. I saw their stark details: the grain of the desiccated wood in the barn, the individual swaying, metronomic heads of the wheat, the sequined rattle of poplar leaves in the bluffs. I could feel the immense weight of the sunlight on it all, which made it seem like the landscape might burst into flames—as indeed it would, later in the fall, when the farmers burned their chaff in great long columns of flame, the smoke rushing off across the fields, then in the evenings hanging in the atmosphere, staining the sunset red. This perfection of weather and crops held within it the apocalypse of flame that I had witnessed so many times in my Meadow Lake years.

In the trunk of the car, stuffed into my suitcase, was a Safeway bag containing Dad's things from the hospital: a shaving kit, a comb, three plums, an orange. He was supposed to eat fruit after his tests, to bring up his blood sugar. Uncle Hank had told me this when he gave me the bag, which had been passed on to him by the hospital officials. He had been the one to give me the news about Dad over the ranger's radio phone, and now he was the bearer of this first physical evidence. He gave it to me without looking at it, and I tried not to look either. I hid it in my luggage. Now it represented an alarming problem: how could I give these things back to Mom?

As we reached the Height of Land, a pang of anxiety gripped me. My stomach shrank into me like a deflating balloon. *Homesick,* I thought. I have all along been homesick, but haven't felt it until now, until I know that my home has unalterably changed, has perhaps even disappeared. I almost pulled over to the side of the road but instead slowed down, kept moving toward the plume of the pulp mill, the gleam of the lake. Alison was nearly asleep beside me and I didn't want to disturb her. We drove past the first of the telecommunications towers, and the town dropped below the tops of the trees as we descended from the peak of the Height of Land.

We passed Alcott Creek with its immense beaver dam on the west side of the road. This was where we used to go to get Christmas trees. We passed logging roads where I had gone partridge hunting with Dad.

Then came the small farms and acreages at the edge of the bush, and finally the town itself. It seemed like nothing had changed. There was the little strip mall, the implement dealership, the KFC where I had worked in high school. I hadn't been home since the previous Christmas—it was the longest I had ever been away from Meadow Lake. Mom and Dad had come to visit us in Ontario just before we moved to Vancouver, but I hadn't seen my home for three seasons.

After the town there was Danilkewich's place, the speed curve, Waddington's and McCrimmon's road, Ratke's place, the seed-cleaning plant, and Bacon's place. And then our place, the farm: a few acres of poplar trees in their full deep greening, with the shadow of a two-storey house shimmering between the leaves. For a moment I was terrified of my own home, didn't know if I could go there. I might instead turn down a side road, go for a drive, wander through the landscape without a destination. But I stayed on the highway, Alison wide awake now, holding my hand, both of us speechless. When we turned in the driveway the first thing I saw was Dad's truck, parked in front of the garage where it always was. We pulled in behind it, and I looked to the house. There at the porch window was Mom's face, disembodied like a ghost, an apparition, a vision. She came out on the front steps and waited for us. She looked half her former size, and she had always been slim. By the time we had reached her, Glenn and Michelle and Bob were there too, and we all stood there beside the petunia bed, hugging and crying and not speaking.

The near bridge at Leonard's Ranch.

THE LONGEST DRIVE

The house was full of people for days—stunned townspeople, relatives, friends who had travelled long distances. The whole town was in shock. Dad had gone golfing three days before he died, and everyone seemed to have seen him out on the course that day. The previous weekend he had played in a tournament and had won the prize for the longest drive.

In addition to this shock there was an incredible outpouring of support from the town. In the eyes of all those people from Meadow Lake, and in their actions, I saw something that made me understand why Mom and Dad lived there. The people know each other in small towns, and while that knowledge can be grating at times, at other times it is the basis of a necessary community support. There were friends, relatives, and neighbours with us for days, cooking and cleaning and talking, just working to keep the household going.

But there was also time to be by ourselves as a family, time to spend with the relatives—eleven of Dad's siblings, all of Mom's siblings, numerous cousins, and close family friends who had always seemed like relatives. And after the hugs and the tears and the outbursts, we became almost comfortable with ourselves. When we were able to speak, we overflowed with stories. There were many tales about Dad—his escapade with the skunk in the garage, his love for lady's slippers, his annual Christmas antics, which involved trying to wind the string of lights around the fifty-foot blue spruce in the front yard. People retold his own stories too: the ones about childhood in Ituna, the one about Grandma driving the car through the back wall and into the living room of their Meadow Lake house, the one about fishing at Cree Lake. Dad was intensely, palpably present. He had become his stories.

He became his place too, as the days went on. He had in fact spent his life becoming this place, and it was only now that we really understood it. We walked down to the barn and leaned on the railings of the corral, thinking of Dad shovelling chop to the bulls, with a cigarette in his bare hand despite the cold, his shoddy grey barn jacket hanging open at the bottom. We walked in the garden, where his prize sunflowers were standing ten and twelve feet high, dozens of them, in full brilliant bloom. Dad had hauled water for them by hand all summer, since the hose wouldn't reach that side of the garden. There were sweet peas and bachelor's buttons and dozens of other flowers, and the vegetables were perfect. It was the time of plenty, the time of harvest. What Mom and Dad had worked for all season.

We also walked out past the granaries and down along the canola field, and in the less dense forest, where dozens of Dad's transplanted spruce trees were now six or seven feet high. The whole place was imprinted with him, and as we walked, separately and in groups, we came to understand the geography of mourning.

The day after the funeral we drove out to Leonard's Ranch, just the six of us, in Dad's truck. We had to take a different route than we used to take, because the closest of the old bridges had been condemned by this time. After taking the detour past Oleksyn's place, we drove into the ranch through an alfalfa field and then stopped at the far side of the old bridge. We stepped warily out onto the ancient tire-path planks, remembering our many terrifying drives over the structure: the breath-holding, the window-rolling, the shrieking to Dad so he would hurry up. I peered over the upriver side at the tremendous pile of brush and garbage that had collected there over the life of the bridge. It seemed to be holding back the water, creating a dam. On the downriver side, the silty water was barely moving.

We took pictures of each other riding the crest of the bridge's most tsunami-like wave, and then we got back in the truck and drove on, past the hired man's house, past the homestead yard (now overgrown, with the red paint bleaching, but the white antlers still as polished as ever), and past the corral. We drove through another gate and down the sandy single-track road, along the clearings where crocuses grow in spring, past the little dugout where I had first fired a gun, and through the gloomy, almost threatening tunnel of the old pine forest, where trees sprouted witches' brooms and other malformations. I had always thought of this as an enchanted forest, and it was the one place on the ranch that I had never really explored.

Past the pine forest was another clearing, the site of most of our birthday wiener roasts in the early years. Our firepits were invisible now, trampled down by the cattle—or more likely by Dad, just before we left each campsite, in his fire-stamping zeal to prevent the Scorcher from striking. There were many cattle, as always—no smarter than before, no more willing to move when the truck approached them, no less curious about this long black creature travelling through their domain. It was like nothing at all had changed, except that Glenn was driving the truck instead of Dad.

We stopped at the far end of the ranch, at the hill with the trenches—the site of our archaeological activities—and we walked down the steep bank carrying bags of food, an axe, a blanket. The trenches were still visible in the ground: low lines that curved along the hillside for forty or fifty yards. We had a wiener roast there, near the base of the steep bank, only a little uphill from the ancient fire ring we had found years before. We chopped our own shallow firepit near a fallen tree, and burned some twigs and deadfall until the fire was hot enough for cooking. From there I could see patches of the river through the clumps of willows that crowded the bank, and I saw the high sand ridges two or three miles away on the other side of the river, where the floodplain gave way to higher ground.

Mom seemed utterly lost in memory for a while. She and Dad used to come to this spot at least once or twice every summer, to have a wiener roast and sit on the fallen log and look out across the floodplain. There was a picture of Dad taken at this spot only a year before, roasting a wiener on a willow stick, gazing into the fire with a look of satisfaction on his face, a sense of utter content and even fascination in the play of the flames. You could tell by the half-smile on his lips that he was humming, as he often did when he was most at peace, most absorbed in the beauties of his world. I could see the memories on Mom's face, the pain of them, the physical force of them. She seemed to be visibly fading away from us, as she sat there on the log and watched us jousting at the fire with our wiener sticks, trying to keep this a happy occasion.

After the coals had died down, Glenn and I poured water on them, jumping back from the simultaneous splash and boom of liquid dropping on embers, the burst of wet ashes into the air. Bob and Michelle shovelled sand over the firepit, and triple-checked, as Dad used to do. Then we packed up the truck and drove across to the Mill Road, and from there turned north over what we have for years called the New Bridge, though it's more than twenty-five years old now.

On the other side we drove through pastures and around the edge of a bog, and we got lost in the willows more than once, but eventually we found the sand hills that I had seen from the far side. They were sand cliffs, really: buttes, islands in a sea of sand and grass. We had come here as kids and had jumped off the lip of the tallest cliff to land in the steeply angled sandbank below. I loved the feeling of weightlessness, the sense of hanging there for a moment before gravity caught me and whipped me down into the soft bed of sand.

I was the first to try it again. I scrambled up the hillside, pulled off my shoes and socks, and leaped off the steepest side. Lift. Flight. I was in the air for so long I lost my balance, waved my arms in circles. My feet kept running in midair, reflexively. When I landed, I skied down the sandy slope for fifteen feet.

"Yeehaw!"

And the competition was on. Longest, highest, most air time. We leaped in tandem, in groups of three. We leaped backwards and in spirals and in pseudo-pike position. Mom sat halfway down the hill and smiled and shook her head. She took pictures of us suspended in the air, with bizarre, distorted expressions on our faces. We leaped and climbed and leaped and climbed until we were giddy and exhausted and, for a brief moment, freed from the burden of our grief.

On our way back to the truck we stopped to look at a cow skeleton, bleached and gleaming in the sand. It had been killed by wolves or cold or disease, probably not too long ago, and it lay there in the sand like something from a photograph of Death Valley. I thought of the caribou skull we had found so many years earlier, wondering if it really had been one after all, or if Dad's imagination had gotten the best of me. No, I remembered the antlers. They were definitely caribou antlers.

I picked up the skull by its eyeholes, examining the shapes of the bone-plates, the jagged meeting places where they seemed to be grafted together. The portholes where major blood vessels had flowed. The teeth that rattled in their sockets. I brushed off the sand on the bottom, held the skull up to my face, and tried to chase after Alison, but I couldn't see around the skull. So instead of chasing I stood there with the skull in front of my face and insisted that she take a picture.

It is on our bookshelf now. Me on the sand, with a ring of hills in the distance, and the head of a nightmare.

The next afternoon Dad's ashes came from the funeral home, and we walked out through the barnyard to the edge of the field and scattered handfuls there. Some of it fell to the earth, and some lifted away in the sky. We each took our turns, solemnly, not speaking, watching the drift of ash in the air. The sun was warm and brilliant as before. That whole time in my memory is saturated with sunlight.

Then we drove out to the pasture, through gates and down a rutted road, past the clumps of wild lady's slippers (not blooming now, but recognizable by their leaves) and willows and many varieties of grasses. In a field beside the pasture was a flock of red-headed sandhill cranes, huge and spindly-legged as storks. I had seen them many times in the air, riding thermals hundreds of feet above us, and had heard their peculiar telephone-like trill, but I had never seen them on the ground. We got out Dad's binoculars and took turns watching them. Each watcher was required to describe their movements, to count and recount the birds, to speculate on how many were males and how many were females.

Then we drove on, through the sea of grass and weeds and goldenrod and thistles with their clumps of white fuzz flying in the breeze. The wind was strong. We stopped in one of Dad's favourite places, near a bluff of thin poplars, and scattered the ashes once again in the wind, lifting our palms upward as if sowing seeds. Some was taken by the wind and some by the soil. The cattle watched us from a distance.

That evening we drove to the lake, and an hour before sunset we paddled out on the water in the boat and the canoe. Dad had gone fishing that spring with Bob at a newly discovered fishing hole that was less than a quarter of a mile from the cabin. After decades of fishing this beautiful but largely infertile lake, we had finally started catching some small pickerel there. Dad had taken out his brand-new rod, received as a birthday present the previous fall and not yet inaugurated. They had let the boat drift as they cast. But before they'd even had a bite, Dad did something uncharacteristic. In one of his mighty, whipping sidearm casts (similar to his tremendous golf swing) he somehow lost his grip and threw the whole fishing outfit—rod, reel, line, super-dude lure—overboard. Bob heard the splash and turned to see the disbelieving look on Dad's face.

"Dairty rotter!" Dad said.

And they spent the rest of the evening fishing not for pickerel but for the lost rod. They dredged the bottom with a heavy lead jig, painstakingly manoeuvring the boat to hold it over the correct spot, since the anchor rope was too short to touch bottom. They hooked clumps of straggly, wiglike weeds, and even a couple of small pickerel, but the rod was never found. Dad blamed the loon shit.

"Probably sunk out of sight in a minute," he said, shaking his head.

But he didn't give up on it. He went out fishing more than usual that summer, and always in the same spot, triangulated between a patch of open beach to the west and a particularly tall cabin to the south. He and Mom caught quite a few fish, but there was no sign of the rod.

It was appropriate that we should go to this spot, marked by Dad's folly and his determination to set it right. So we paddled slowly over there, set our bearings by the familiar landmarks, and again took turns scattering ashes into the water. We could see the pieces sinking, like reverse smoke. Some particles sank faster than others. I thought of *The Tempest*: "Full fathom five thy father lies." We had returned him to earth, to air, to water. And also to fire.

When we were finished we sat there calmly for a long while, staring down into the placid surface, the water so clear we could see more than thirty feet down. But here it was deeper than that, and the clarity gave only a sharper view into darkness. I thought about all our fishing trips with Dad, all our time spent on the water, looking down into murkier depths than these, wondering what was down there. The only sound was the rhythm of the boats nudging each other. I looked further over the edge of the canoe and saw myself peeking up from the depths. I looked old, wrinkled. Some day I too would be down there, part of the water.

"Well," Mom said after a while. "Are we gonna fish or what?"

So we took our rods from the boat bottoms and readied the lures, and cast out, one at a time, around the boats. *Plip, plip, plip, plip, plip, plip*, the jigs sounded as they broke the surface and shimmied their way to the bottom.

"Two bits for the first fish," I said. Dad had always been the one to say this.

"Four bits for a Daiwa rod and reel," Glenn added.

In half an hour, we had enough pickerel for the next day's breakfast.

St. Cyprien Cemetery.

OLD CEMETERY

When I got back to Vancouver, I found at the bottom of my suitcase the bag of fruit that Uncle Hank had given me. The plums were mouldy but the orange looked fine. I sat on the bed and bit open a flap of the peel, then pressed a thumb in and unwrapped the inner fruit. I ate it, section by section, looking around the cluttered room, thinking: Dad never even got to see where we live.

It is difficult to grieve in a new place. Sometimes I could fool myself into thinking that I was the only one who had gone away. For Mom, immersed in the surroundings she had shared with Dad for more than twenty years, there was no possibility of such self-deception. The farm was saturated with memories, both comforting and painful. Each new increment of the season brought with it the reminders of other seasons. Each day was an anniversary of something: the last time Mom and Dad had gone partridge hunting, the last time they had seen the lilacs blooming, the last time they had harvested cucumbers from the garden. Sometimes when I was back home I saw the strain of memory on Mom's face: a sudden stricken look, as if memory was an electric charge.

Glenn had moved out to the farm to help her with the work and to keep her company, but I knew no one could help her with the memories.

I came back at Thanksgiving, and again in December and February. It wasn't enough. The time between my visits felt like a different life altogether. Whenever I got back home I was overwhelmed by the place and the memories that were waiting there for me. It was no longer just home; it was also the scene of a vague and inescapable fear.

Still, not everything had changed. When I came back we wandered in the usual places, remembering all the times we had spent there. One of my favourite things to do in the winter was to feed Dad's pheasants, the beautiful ringnecks that had matured over the summer into magnificent creatures with an opalescent sheen on their feathers. Dad had intended to release them out at the pasture that fall, but then after he died Mom wasn't able to do it right away, and by Thanksgiving the snow had already come and she didn't think they would be able to accustom themselves to the wild before the winter set in. So she kept them until spring.

The pheasants had been Dad's pride and joy in the last few months of his life. He had bought them, like so many other things, on a whim. We had stopped raising chickens and turkeys many years before, but one day when Mom and Dad were coming back from Edmonton, they saw a roadside sign that said "Pheasant chicks" and they stopped in at the pheasant farm. They got home with a dozen tiny ring-necked pheasants, and they raised them as we had done with the chickens, first under a heat lamp in our old garbage shack and then in the run-down chicken coop behind the barn. Dad loved to stand and watch them, and he paraded every visitor out past the bull pen to view his marvels of nature. They were incredibly skittish, however, and would explode into flight at the slightest movement, sometimes injuring themselves against the windows of the chicken coop. Dad whispered as he slowly opened the door, and he spoke to them in a low, soothing voice. Then he stood completely still and watched as the birds came out of their hiding places to peck at the grain or the alfalfa he had brought.

Pheasants are not native to northern Saskatchewan, but Dad had often talked about releasing a few of them up there to see how they would do. He had even tried it once before, but with only two birds, which both turned out to be males. They hung around the farm for more than a year, often standing in the tall plants in the middle of the garden, crowing their distinctive note that sounds like a rusty screen door. But after the second winter they disappeared. It was probably no coincidence that a family of foxes moved in under one of our granaries at around that time.

But even after that failure, Dad had maintained that it was possible to establish a group of pheasants in the north, and with this new flock of birds he was sure he would succeed. His plans were nearly foiled again by the local fox family, but after Glenn travelled back to the hatchery to bring in reinforcements, there were still nine birds left by mid-August.

It wasn't until early spring that Mom and Glenn let them out of the coop, not by taking them down to the pasture— because they feared the birds would hurt themselves during the drive—but simply by opening the door and standing back.

The pheasants stepped out tentatively, one at a time, onto the newly thawed ground, and then took noisily to the air.

They didn't go far that summer. We heard the males crowing in the garden most mornings until midsummer, and often we saw them huddling under the caraganas and the spruce trees. After a while we didn't see the females, and we hoped that meant they were tending their new broods of young ones. But as the summer progressed, we spotted the birds less often, and we speculated that they must have wandered farther afield, perhaps in search of water. We heard reports of them sometimes. One had been killed on the highway, and another had been seen at the edge of the bush near our neighbour's place.

Over the winter there was no sign of them, though we had expected that. It was the following spring when we listened again for them crowing in the garden. But we didn't hear it. Eventually we had to admit that the pheasants were all gone, that they must not have belonged so far north after all.

Even so, there were still some surprises. Nearly two years after the birds had been released, Bob was driving the snowmobile out by the south end of our fields and he saw what he swore was a pheasant, flying up out of the bush and sailing along beside him for a few seconds. Later that winter, Mom was out snowshoeing east of the house when she found two large patches of swooping, curved marks in the snow, with no tracks leading toward them or away. The calligraphy of wingtips. They might have been partridges, but we liked to think that a pair of Dad's pheasants had returned.

In the summer, the garden was always a source of memories. I walked there by myself one June morning and remembered

Mom and Dad's daily noon-hour perambulations. "Let's go for a stroll, love," he would say, after five minutes of slurping soup, and off they would go, Mom in her rubber boots and Dad in his "garden shoes," which were old dress shoes that had been so trampled down at the heel that they looked like German clogs. They wandered along the flowerbeds beside the house and then out through the many rows of the garden, Dad watering his beloved cucumbers, checking the growth of each tendril, appraising the progress of each flower. He would be singing to himself, "Pa pum pum" and "Huh hummm," watching for robins and hummingbirds, bending to uproot quackgrass and creeping charlie and sowthistle, tossing the weeds over his shoulder to drop like paratroopers in the grass. Deadheading petunias. Cradling the blossom of a clematis, a gladiolus, a sweet pea or a rare rose, and bending down to inhale its soft breath.

Mom has kept up with the garden on her own, but it has been too much work for her. The whole farm is too much work. Even though Glenn lives there and helps out as much as he can, we all know that someday she will have to leave the farm. None of us wants to think about this, but we silently acknowledge the truth of it. Eventually the farm will no longer be ours. And I wonder: what will become of Dad then? What will become of all our memories?

The last time I was home, I drove by our old house in town, as I always do. But this time I was surprised to see a For Sale sign on the front lawn. I stopped the car there in the middle of my old street and looked at the house, wondering who was moving away. I had no idea who lived there anymore, and there was no evidence of anyone in the house, even though it was Christmastime. On the spot where our garden used to be, there was now a two-car garage. All the towering Russian poplar trees on the north side of the house had been felled.

I was tempted to pose as a buyer, just to get another look at the place, to see if anything remained from my memories. Was the old pool table still downstairs? We'd had to leave it down there when we moved out, because it wouldn't fit out through the renovations. What about the little milk-bottle door where glass jars of two-percent used to appear without warning, and where we used to wriggle in and out of the house to avoid using the regular door? I wondered if Pierre's scratch marks were still there on the doorframe, from the times when he had begged to go outside.

Probably none of it was there. Probably I would only be disillusioned by the lack of connection between the place and my memory.

I felt a vague attachment to the house and the neighbourhood, but it wasn't a visceral connection, a homing instinct. It was filtered through years of memory and years of change, so that the old house had become little more than a symbol of my childhood, an empty structure to be furnished with stories. *And you grew like quackgrass in the backyard.* Maybe someday this is how I will feel about the farm and about Meadow Lake itself. If Mom moves to the city, as she sometimes talks about doing, then I wonder if I will return physically to Meadow Lake—if I can't drive up the driveway of the farm and walk down to the barnyard and look out over the fields.

Maybe it doesn't matter. Somehow it will always be my place, just as it is Dad's place, and the place of the Honsbergers, and Cup Warren, and all the unknown people before them. I like to think that the land doesn't forget, that our stories echo somewhere around our places, and that it only takes an inquisitive soul to come along and listen for them.

Yes: places have voices. I listen more carefully than I used to. I seek them out, especially the ones that might have been forgotten. Last summer I learned about one such place in the heart of my hometown.

I was looking through some old local-history documents in the Meadow Lake Museum, and as I was reading about Father Cochin's founding of the first school, I found a hand-drawn map of the early settlement, made probably by a junior high school student in the fifties. The old school site was marked there, but what surprised me was another square of land not far from the lake, which was labelled "Old Cemetery."

I had never heard of any cemetery other than the one out by Highway 4, where we had placed a memorial marker for Dad that spring, and where Grandma Laliberte's second husband was buried. I thought surely I would have known about another graveyard in town, but I asked Mom about it when I got home for lunch, and she said, "Oh yeah, there is one, down by the golf course, toward the lake. Dad went out there once, I remember, but I didn't go with him."

I clarified my directions and that afternoon I drove out to the golf course road, and then east along a narrow dirt track to a hay field. A sign at the gate read Cemetery Traffic Only.

I looked out across the windswept field and saw in the distance a thin white cross at the top of a little hill. I had driven past this place hundreds of times but had never noticed the cross. It was probably visible from the golf course clubhouse.

There was a single-track road through the field, much like the one at Leonard's Ranch, and I drove slowly along it, the bristles of cut hay scraping and clattering against the undercarriage of the car. The sunlight streaked down through the fast-moving clouds, and I could see shadows rushing across the hill where the graveyard was. In the middle distance was the lake, with its lines of muddy whitecaps stacking up against the near shore, and in the far distance was the omnipresent blue line of the Height of Land. This place, certainly, was part of the original meadow, the one that had given the area so many of its names. I felt unaccountably like I was visiting the oldest part of my home, the place with the most history, the most voices.

I had to walk the last quarter mile because recent flooding had covered the trail. Across the damp field, the cemetery looked like an island. There was a single tree in the middle, and the one tall white cross that I had seen from the road, and a few small grave markers scattered within the precincts of a wire fence. I learned later that it was called St. Cyprien Cemetery, after Cyprien Morin, the great patriarch of the Metis in Lac des Prairies. It had been built on Cyprien's land, and he was buried there too.

Most of the grave markers were either gone or were so worn out that none of the names were legible, but just inside the gate there was a plaque that looked to be of recent construction, containing the names and dates of all the people interred there. The dates of death went from 1909 to 1935. The names were familiar ones: Murray, Morin, Bear, Laliberte, Matchee. In the first decade of the cemetery, virtually all of them were Cree and Metis names, and most of these families still lived in the area. By the early twenties, the Scottish names and the Slavic names began to appear.

The ages were marked there too, and the numbers told a grim story. Many of the dead were children, and only a few had lived beyond sixty.

So many stories could be constructed around a date, a name, a place. I imagined the hardship of living and working day after day in such a harsh climate: the toll of accident and disease, the lack of medical help. In November of 1918 there was a long list of children who had died within a few days of each other. Probably the Spanish flu epidemic. Even this place, so far from the rest of the world, was fatally connected to it.

As I walked between the uneven rows and looked out into the windy field toward the lake, I thought of Dad walking in this same place on that unknown day in the past. He would have wandered here, humming and listening, perhaps kneeling down to examine the illegible inscription of a gravestone. I wondered what stories he told himself about these people and their place. For a moment, I thought I could hear his voice.

ACKNOWLEDGMENTS

Warmest thanks to Denise Bukowski for knowing there was a story here, and to Martha Kanya-Forstner for her faith, patience, and miraculous editorial perceptiveness.

For assistance with research I am indebted to the Meadow Lake Library, the Meadow Lake Museum and Historical Society, the *Meadow Lake Progress*, the North Battleford Court of Queen's Bench Records Office, the Saskatchewan Archives Board for access to Frank Crean's photos, and the Saskatchewan Arts Board for a grant to research the Great Fire of 1919. I also gratefully acknowledge the institutional support of the University of British Columbia Department of English, the University of Manitoba Institute for the Humanities, and the University of Saskatchewan Department of English. Thanks especially to colleagues Bill New, Sherrill Grace, Laurie Ricou, Arlene Young, Natalie Johnson, Fred Cutler, and Len Findlay. Thanks also to Marlow Esau for his stampede photo, and to Robert Thacker for introducing me to the poems of Kim Stafford. Thank you, Marilyn Dumont and everyone at Sage Hill, for showing me that language is electricity.

Love to Alison, my first listener, first reader, and altogether first in everything. Love and thanks to Mom, Glenn, Michelle, and Bob for their unflagging support and good humour, and to the rest of my multiplicitous family, for remembering. Thanks, Dad, for the stories, which are everything. And to all the other storytellers of northern Saskatchewan, who have immeasurably enriched my life, I offer my sincere admiration and gratitude.

Dad at Cree Lake.

ABOUT THE AUTHOR

Warren Cariou taught Aboriginal literature at the University of British Columbia and now teaches at the University of Manitoba. His first book, *The Exalted Company of Roadside Martyrs: Two Novellas*, garnered rave reviews. He lives in Winnipeg.